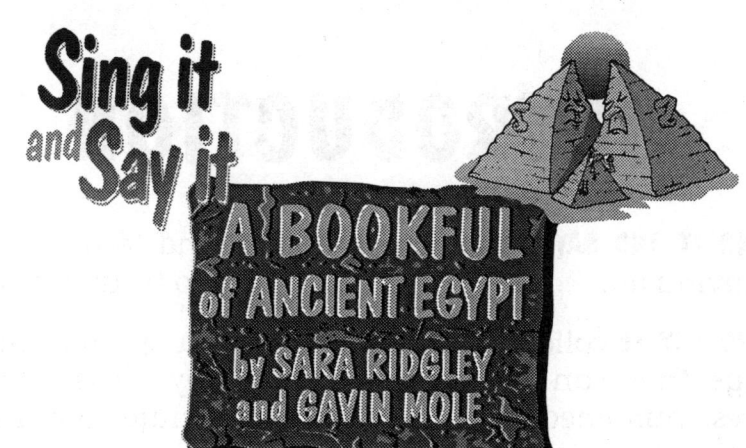

CONTENTS

	page
NILE STYLE Follow the Nile through southern Egypt to Tutankhamun's tomb, jazzing with Cairo Kyle the Crocodile along the way!	3
LAND OF THE SUN GOD Travel from the Valley of the Kings to the temple of Re at Karnak, survive a Nile flood and meet a scribbling scribe!	45
THE PYRAMID FILE Journey up the Nile to Giza, meet One Hungry Mummy, Sandy Syd, a lonely little pyramid, dancing slaves and the Jinxed Sphinx!	87

Series Editor: Mark Mumford

Music processed by Barnes Music Engraving Ltd
East Sussex TN22 4HA, England

Cover Design by Paul Clark Designs

Exclusive distributors:

International Music Publications Limited
Southend Road, Woodford Green, Essex IG8 8HN

International Music Publications Limited
25 rue d'Hauteville, 75010 Paris, France

Danmusik
Vognmagergade 7, DK-1120 Copenhagen K, Denmark

International Music Publications GmbH Germany
Marstallstrasse 8, D-80539 München, Germany

Warner Bros Publications Inc
145800 NW 48th Avenue, PO Box 4340, Miami, Florida 33014, USA

Nuova Carisch S.P.A.
Via M. F. Quintiliano 40, 20138 Milano, Italy

Warner/Chappell Music Inc, Australia
1 Cassins Avenue, North Sydney, New South Wales 2060, Australia

Published 1997

INTRODUCTION

Welcome to **SING IT AND SAY IT (Can anyone play it?)** and to a new way of learning, teaching and having fun – and no, you don't have to be able to read music.

Each **SING IT AND SAY IT** collection concentrates on a specific subject and offers a variety of songs that can be used in day-to-day class work, performed as individual pieces, combined to make three ten-minute mini-musicals or linked together to create a thirty-minute show.

For easy and practical teaching, the book has been divided into three sections, clearly identifying each mini-musical. Director's Notes and song lyrics for each section are grouped together. They come first each time, followed by the complete musical score for the section, making continuous playing easier.

The songs are packed with lively lyrics, guaranteed to appeal to the children of today. They are easy to teach and fun to learn with music that is catchy, memorable and full of character.

The audio tape to accompany the book is both a performance (including voices) and a backing track (without voices), so **SING IT AND SAY IT** gives you musicians and singers to help you on your way.

The Director's Notes are a complete 'selection box' of suggestions. They will help to add a real cross-curricular flavour to both classroom activities and complete stage performances. Drama, instrumental accompaniments, sound effects, costume, art and craft and topic ideas will all combine to make **SING IT AND SAY IT** an experience packed with learning and laughter.

Throughout the book we've used the following symbols and titles to help you find your way around:

 **SING IT.**    **DRAMA.**    **ARTS & CRAFTS.**

 **SAY IT.**    **SOUND EFFECTS. (FX.)**    **TOPICS ARISING.**

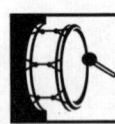 **PLAY IT.**

SING IT AND SAY IT has been created by Sara and Gavin to bring entertainment into education for both children and teachers. Enjoy it!

ACKNOWLEDGEMENTS

Heartfelt thanks to Cheron Mole (tolerance, musical skill, great lunches), Joyce and Ed Woodwark (financial help, boundless enthusiasm), Andy Spiller (inspiration in the recording studio), the fabulous **SING IT AND SAY IT** Gang (for the audio cassette), and Teg and Ivor Evans (for the **SING IT AND SAY IT** Wing)!

Look out for other titles in the **SING IT AND SAY IT** series. See back cover or check with your local dealer for details.

1 NILE STYLE

CONTENTS

	Director's Notes	Musical Score
SING IT AND SAY IT	4	23
RIVER NILE	6	25
DESERT GOLD	8	26
NORTH WITH THE NILE	10	31
INTO THE LIGHT	12	32
TUTANKHAMUN	14	33
AFTERLIFE DREAM	16	35
CAIRO KYLE THE CROCODILE	18	39
SING IT AND SAY IT (FINALE)	20	43
GLOSSARY	21	

This **SING IT AND SAY IT** episode introduces us to the grand old **RIVER NILE**, flowing past Ramses tomb at Abu Simbel to meet the Pharoah's slave miners digging for treasure in **DESERT GOLD**. We travel **NORTH WITH THE NILE** to go **INTO THE LIGHT** with **TUTANKHAMUN** and share in the splendours of his tomb in **AFTERLIFE DREAM**, then stomp our way through a Saturday night with jazz musician **CAIRO KYLE THE CROCODILE** and his boys, before a rousing **SING IT AND SAY IT** finale. Our journey into ancient Egypt has begun!

CAST LIST

SING IT AND SAY IT	**Solo:** teacher, the one in charge (well, almost) **Ensemble:** everybody join in!
RIVER NILE	**Ensemble:** introducing us to the great river of Egypt **Backing Singers:** er – singing the backing **Solo:** the Nile, performing his verse with flow and style
DESERT GOLD	**Ensemble:** two groups of tired slaves in the Pharoah's mine **Solo:** strict Overseer, encouraging the slaves to dig
NORTH WITH THE NILE	**Backing Singers:** ah-ing splendidly **Solo:** the Nile, leading us to the Valley of the Kings
INTO THE LIGHT	**Ensemble:** rejoicing as the Pharoah enters the Next World **Backing Singers:** adding to the celebrations
TUTANKHAMUN	**Solo:** telling Tutankhamun's tale **Backing Singers:** with very easy words
AFTERLIFE DREAM	**Solo:** praising the rich scenes in Pharoah's tomb
CAIRO KYLE THE CROCODILE	**Solo:** Cairo Kyle, fatherly trombone-playing Nile reptile **Solo:** Big Boy Miles, teeth-snapping son of Cairo Kyle **Solo:** Baby Giles, sousaphone-playing younger brother **Ensemble:** with snappy chorus lines
SING IT AND SAY IT (FINALE)	**Solo:** teacher, the one in charge (well, almost) **Chorus:** everybody join in!

SING IT AND SAY IT

DIRECTOR'S NOTES

Our first song expresses the essence of the **SING IT AND SAY IT** project:

SING IT. Singing easy-to-learn music
SAY IT. Saying entertaining words with rhyme and rhythm
PLAY IT. Playing simple accompaniments

We'd add **BUILDING** to that list. Building confidence, vocabulary and musical ability. Building concentration and timing, teamwork and, discipline.

The other word which encapsulates **SING IT AND SAY IT** is FUN. Fun in learning *and* fun in teaching.

 **SING IT.** The first and last sections of this song are identical for easy learning and, the whole song is repeated at the end of this 10-minute episode.

 **SING IT.** **SING IT AND SAY IT** can be performed as an ensemble, in separate groups or as a solo.

 **FX.** Clapping and clicking of fingers will find their natural places in this song.

 **DRAMA.** However you use the material, your class will have plenty of suggestions for actions and simple dance routines. **PLAY IT** may inspire actions like miming a trombone player, pianist or guitarist. Someone will want to conduct the class and everyone will want to shout 'Four!' (after 'One, Two, Three').

 **SAY IT.** Audition for a natural leader to take the part of teacher. Oh, you want to do it? Go on, then.

| THE SONG |

 **SING IT.**

ENSEMBLE: Sing it and say it, can anyone play it?
There's no need to be shy.
Sing it and say it, can anyone play it?
Come on, let's give it a try.

You'll soon learn the tune in a jiff and a half,
You'll soon learn the words, they might make you laugh!
So listen to me, there's no need to read,
Rhyme and rhythm are all you need –

 **SAY IT.**

TEACHER: Sing it with me on the count of three –
One, two, three . . .

ENSEMBLE: *(shouted)* Four!

 **SING IT.**

ENSEMBLE: Sing it and say it, can anyone play it?
There's no need to be shy.
Sing it and say it, can anyone play it?
Come on, let's give it a try.

| MUSICAL SCORE – page 23 |

RIVER NILE

DIRECTOR'S NOTES

Welcome to ancient Egypt. **SING IT AND SAY IT** style! Our guide to this book is the life-force of Egypt, the River Nile.

 **SING IT.** Unlimited numbers of ensemble introduce the river in rousing style. Then the Nile himself (or herself) sings us a fact-packed verse. My, my, the backing singers have a tricky task. *Ah . . .*

 **SAY IT.** If you prefer, divide the class into groups and speak all or part of the lyric for a different dramatic effect.

 **DRAMA.** Cast a strong character for the Nile. How would the class describe the river? Majestic? Slick? Clever? How old is he? Which famous human does he most resemble? Ransack your pupils' brains for costuming suggestions.

 **TOPIC.** The Nile, the world's longest river. Dribbling out of Lake Victoria as a trainee stream, he becomes the White Nile, flows north for 6695 km (4160 miles), then drops gratefully into the Mediterranean after spreading his irrigational favours through desert and delta.

 **ART & CRAFT.** Organise a work-party to make a large scale Africa map. Add Lake Victoria, bordered by Tanzania to the south, Kenya to the east and Uganda to the west. Add Rwanda, Burundi and Zaire, home of another great African river, the Congo (now the Zaire). Add two further wonderfully-named waterways: the Zambezi and the Limpopo. Paint wallcharts of vegetation and wildlife found in the river valleys. Which creatures live in the rivers, on the banks or up in the trees?

 **ART & CRAFT.** On your Africa map, draw in Egypt's straight borders. Add Abu Simbel at the southern end of Lake Nasser on the western banks of the river and the gold mines opposite, in the Eastern Desert – they're our first port of call.

 **FX.** Watery noises – if you must!

THE SONG

 **SING IT.**

		BACKING SINGERS
ENSEMBLE:	River Nile,	
	River Nile,	
	From his source on a course	Ah
	Of over four thousand miles, he	
	Ripples and he roars,	Ah
	And then rests for a while.	
	He's a	
	River with style, the	Ah
	Great River Nile.	Great River Nile
NILE:	Lake Vic-	
	-toria's home,	Ah
	My birthplace, my source,	
	Through the	
	Desert I flow	Ah
	On a northerly course.	
	Through Su-	
	-dan into Egypt, I	Ah
	Broaden and swell as I	Ah
	Glide past the gold mines,	Ah
	Near Abu Simbel.	

MUSICAL SCORE – page 25

DESERT GOLD

DIRECTOR'S NOTES

A dramatic number, building in intensity to keep your audience enthralled!

 **SING IT.** The digging chorus has a solid beat and the whole song has a 'chain-gang' feel.

 **SAY IT.** The "Shh!" is a Whisper It. The slaves' "Dig, Dig!" is a Say It or Shout It. Add a Scream It to follow the whipcrack if you must.

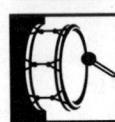 **PLAY IT.** Cymbal, crashed with intensity.

 **DRAMA.** Cast as many slaves as you can. Resist the temptation to give the Headmaster the part of lash-cracking Overseer.

 **TOPIC.** Gold. Nuggets of the priceless metal were melted, hammered and moulded into magnificent death-masks with glittering obsidian and crystal eyes or sarcophagi (inner coffins) to protect the Pharoah's mummified corpse. Goldsmiths worked by the eerie glow of flickering furnaces to produce rings for the Pharoah's fingers and toes, dazzling necklaces inlaid with turquoise, bracelets set with green malachite, amulets to ward off evil, figurines of the gods and heavy pectoral collars to wear across the chest, hung with carved gold falcons. It's a wonder any of them could stand up, wearing that lot!

 **ART & CRAFT.** Design gold jewellery using metallic pens or acrylic paints. Copy Egypt's favourite colour schemes: bright blue lapis lazuli, flame-red Carnelian, greeny-blue turquoise, black obsidian.

 **TOPIC.** Look further at the gemstones used in ancient Egypt. Study raw and polished chunks. Carnelian can be gathered on beaches around British coasts, especially on eastern and north-eastern shores. Obsidian, gleaming jet-black with a gold sheen glinting in the light, is often turned into polished eggs. Jasper and agate come in a rainbow of colours. Turquoise and silver were a favourite combination of the Incas and are still widely used in Mexican jewellery. Investigate craft fairs, the Natural History Museum or a gem and rock shop for samples.

 **TOPIC.** Trade. Gold was made into precious gifts for merchants and the Pharoah's representatives to take to other countries within Africa and overseas, to exchange for ivory and silver, horses and copper, spices and iron. It was used to buy princesses from the King of Babylon – destined to be brides of the Pharoah. Cedar was purchased from the Lebanon with gold bracelets, then the aromatic wood was carved into scented caskets to be placed in the Pharoah's tomb, filled with treasure made from – yes, you guessed it – gold.

 **FX.** Metallic digging sounds. The crack of the Overseer's lash.

THE SONG

 **SING IT.**

SLAVES GROUP 1:	Dig, dig, dig, dig, dig, dig, dig.
SLAVES GROUP 2:	We've been digging down a gold mine.
SLAVES GROUP 1:	Dig, dig.
SLAVES GROUP 2:	We've been working underground.
SLAVES GROUP 1:	Dig, dig.
SLAVES GROUP 2:	We've been searching for a long time.
SLAVES GROUP 1:	Dig, dig.
SLAVES GROUP 2:	Shall we tell you what we've found?
SLAVES GROUP 1:	Sshh!
SLAVES GROUP 2:	It's a seam of gold so rich and old,
	With nuggets by the barrowload,
	Increasing by a thousandfold,
	Our Pharoah's wealth, or so we're told.
ALL SLAVES:	But we're all slaves and slaves are sold for gold.
ALL SLAVES:	Our Pharoah's face will form the mould,
	To make his mask of solid gold,
	The gold is melted, poured and rolled,
	Inscribed with spells and songs and odes.
	But we're all slaves and slaves are sold for gold.
SLAVES GROUP 1:	Dig, dig,
SLAVES GROUP 2:	We've been digging down a gold mine.
SLAVES GROUP 1:	Dig, dig.
SLAVES GROUP 2:	We've been working underground.
SLAVES GROUP 1:	Dig, dig.
SLAVES GROUP 2:	We've been searching for a long time.
SLAVES GROUP 1:	Dig, dig.
OVERSEER:	Don't you tell them what we've found!
SLAVES GROUP 1:	Sshh!

		SLAVES
OVERSEER:	You jeweller slaves	
	Do as you're told or	
	I will scream and	Ah
	I will scold, you	Ah
	Don't have long, the	Ah
	Pharoah's old, no	Ah
	Overtime, just	Ah
	Overload,	Ah
	'Cause you're all slaves	
	And slaves are sold for *(whipcrack)* . . . gold!	

MUSICAL SCORE – page 26

NORTH WITH THE NILE

DIRECTOR'S NOTES

A reprise (well, same music, different words) of part of the opening number to sing whilst we travel upriver.

 **TOPIC.** The Temples of Ramses II, also known as Ramses the Great. He lived for 67 years and built more monuments than any other Pharoah. Must have had pals in the Planning Department! His Great Temple at Abu Simbel knocks the senses sideways with its four massive statues of the Pharoah, 22 metres (over 70 feet) high – a national landmark featured on the back of an Egyptian pound note. Ramses built his edifice and the nearby Temple of Hathor (goddess of beauty and happiness, often portrayed as a cow, poor dear) over 3200 years ago and they are of such national and world importance that, when the waters of Lake Nasser rose and threatened the Temples, an international rescue effort was mounted and these huge buildings were moved, block, rock and statue to safer high ground.

On 22 February, Egypt celebrates Ramses' ascension to the throne. He gave orders that his Great Temple was built so that on this date, the sun would dance on his statue inside the Inner Temple, making it appear alive. It used to happen on 21 February, Ramses' birthday, but when the building was moved, the day shifted by one. That's removal men for you!

 **SING IT.** Dust off your "Ah"s, Backing Singers.

 **ARTS & CRAFT.** Let's splash a bit more water on our Africa map. Add the River Niger, rising close to the source of the River Senegal and flowing into the Gulf of Guinea at the Bight of Benin; the River Orange rising in the High Veld at Africa's tip and meeting the Atlantic at the Cape of Good Hope and the marvellously-named River Oubangi, appearing in Nile country near Lake Victoria and irrigating Zaire.

 **TOPIC.** The Nile flows for almost 1000 km (620 miles) of its length inside Egypt, reaching Luxor, ancient Thebes, 675 km (420 miles) south of Cairo. The name Luxor derives from *El-Oksor*, Arabic for 'the palaces'. Old Thebes was Egypt's glittering city for four centuries, its streets described in the Iliad as places where 'heaps of precious ingots gleam'. Obelisks of silver, ivory and alabaster dazzled in the sun and the impressive Temple of Luxor was once reached by a Sphinx-lined avenue.

 **ART & CRAFT.** Make clay figurines of Ramses and smaller models of his wife Nefertari and their children. In Egyptian sculpture and painting, the Pharoah was always the largest figure and his family, advisors and servants were shown as disproportionately tiny people. Wives stood knee-high, children gathered at ankle level in some cases, like miniature aliens. (Now, there's a thought!) Some say the pyramids were early space stations, to quote some theories . . . but, more of this later.

THE SONG

 **SING IT.**

		BACKING SINGERS
NILE:	Far away from the splendour	
	Of Ramses' tomb,	
	Lined with paintings of battles	
	In Ramses' room, past	
	Luxor, or Thebes, as the	Ah
	City was known, to the	Ah
	Valley of Kings,	Ah
	Home of Tutankhamun.	Tutankhamun

MUSICAL SCORE – page 31

INTO THE LIGHT

DIRECTOR'S NOTES

A short, but impressive song with a distinct air of majesty.

SING IT. The vocal harmony is not what you might expect, but the result is well worth the effort. Take a breath for each line and an extra-deep breath before the final word, 'death', sing it loud and sing it long to mark the fact that the end of a mortal lifetime was a celebration in ancient Egypt – the release of a person's Ka (life force) and the start of a magnificent journey into the afterlife.

PLAY IT. Cymbals, majestically crashed – and if you've got a gong, give it a go! Listen to the tape for regal inspiration.

DRAMA. If possible, use simple lighting to stage dusk, then darkness falling on the Pharoah's subjects as they keep their overnight vigil. Then use a bright stage to represent a hot Egyptian dawn as the Pharoah finally shuffles off his gold-plated papyrus sandals.

TOPIC. Legend has it that Re, the sun god and bringer of life, entered the sky at sunrise to lead the Pharoah into the afterlife, so dying at dawn was highly recommended! The Pharoah then became a god, part of the holy family of Re which included his children Tefnut, god of moisture and rain, and Shu, god of the air and atmosphere. Start a Re family tree with sun designs (see **Journey of the Sun God** in the next episode for more Re-velations!)

ART & CRAFT. Try making a star curtain or night sky backdrop. See **SING IT AND SAY IT, A Bookful of Ancient Greece** for a song called **Heroes of the Heavens** for extra ideas. Black net works well, hung with silver paper circles and star shapes. Cut up old Easter egg boxes or sparkly Christmas cards and glittery wrapping paper.

TOPIC. The story of Seth. Here's a good tale to read aloud: Seth was a god to fear. In charge of dry-baked deserts and wicked sandstorms, he was also god of evil. Brother of Osiris, Lord of the Underworld, Seth was a jealous soul. He invited Osiris to a feast, fought and overpowered him, hacked him into 14 pieces, locked the dismembered body inside a cedar chest and threw it into the Nile. Isis, beautiful wife of Osiris, found it and employed a team of skilled seamstresses to stitch her husband back together. The scarred body of poor Osiris was anointed with healing balms and oils, wrapped in bandages and restored to full health. Still in fear of evil old Seth, Isis raised her baby son, Horus in total secrecy, but when he reached adult god-hood, Horus fought his uncle Seth and defeated him.

Throughout Egypt a magic amulet, the Eye of Horus, is still widely used as a good luck charm, painted on boats and worn as a piece of jewellery to protect against the power of Seth. Horus is a sky god, a hawk high in the heavens with the sun and moon for eyes, whose name means 'he who is far above'.

THE SONG

 **SING IT.**

		BACKING SINGERS
ENSEMBLE:	The sky grows	Ah
	Dark, the stars stand	Ah
	Still, the heavens	Ah
	Hold their breath.	Hold their breath
	The people	Ah
	Sing, the people	Ah
	Sigh, the people	Ah
	Pray to Seth.	Pray to Seth
	A burst of	Ah
	Light, the sun so	Ah
	Bright sees Pharoah	Ah
	Draw a breath.	Draw a breath
	The Next World	Ah
	Calls, The Pharoah	Ah
	Smiles, the god-king	Ah
	Welcomes death.	Welcomes death

MUSICAL SCORE – page 32

TUTANKHAMUN

DIRECTOR'S NOTES

A simple song with charm, outlining the tale of the boy-king.

 **SING IT.** This can be performed as a round with five groups taking a couplet each, but if that presents too many problems, sing just the top line, as in the score.

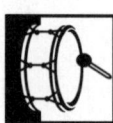 **PLAY IT.** Triangle to the fore!

 **DRAMA.** Stage this song simply and seriously for the most impressive and dramatic effect.

 **TOPIC.** Tutankhamun. Ask the class to imagine what it would be like to become King of Egypt as a very young boy. What responsibilities would you have? Who would report to you? Who would advise you? Egyptian society resembled a pyramid: on the pinnacle, the Pharoah. Below him, an elite strata of the Grand Vizier, chief government officials, noblemen, high priests and priestesses. Then the scribes and minor priests and below them the craftsmen – stonemasons, potters, jewellers, goldsmiths. Forming the base of the pyramid was a workforce of servants, labourers, slaves and peasants.

When he died in his late teens, Tutankhamun was a husband and father of two daughters, both sadly stillborn. He was possibly the son, possibly the half-brother of Akenaten (also known as King Amenhotep IV) whose wife was the famously stunning Nefertiti. Whether or not she was Tutankhamun's mum is a matter for debate – are you still with us? Either way, Tutankhamun's wife was Nefertiti's daughter, Ankhsenamon.

Tutankhamun was responsible for reinstating Amon-Re (or just plain Re) as the main deity of Egypt after Akenaten's defection to rival god, Aten, seen by many as an act of horrendous hypocrisy. So much so that statues of Akenaten were deliberately destroyed or defaced and records of much of his reign were obliterated from the face of history.

 **ART & CRAFT.** Make papier mâché masks in rich golds and lapis lazuli blues. Use coloured glass nuggets or painted pebbles for eyes. Add the false beard of Pharoah indicating that the monarch was indeed a god (even worn by the ladies who held the post, such as Queen Hatshepsut, a woman of great determination who ruled Egypt for 20 years). The vulture on Tutankhamun's head-dress represented power over Upper Egypt and the cobra meant he also ruled Lower Egypt. See **Afterlife Dream** and **Valley of the Kings** for more data on Tutankhamun.

THE SONG

 **SING IT.**

		BACKING SINGERS
SOLO:	Tutankhamun, Tutankhamun.	
	Died so young, Died so young.	Tutankhamun Tutankhamun
	It's so sad, It's so sad.	Tutankhamun Tutankhamun
	King of ancient Egypt, King of ancient Egypt.	Tutankhamun Tutankhamun
	Just a boy, Just a boy.	Tutankhamun Tutankhamun
		Tutankhamun Tutankhamun

MUSICAL SCORE – page 33

AFTERLIFE DREAM

DIRECTOR'S NOTES

A haunting song, inspired by a painting in Tutankhamun's tomb.

 **SING IT.** This is a beautiful song for a clear single voice. Use groups or ensemble if you prefer.

 **SAY IT.** Use the lyrics as a poem in class work.

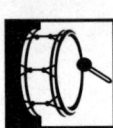 **PLAY IT.** Tinkle that triangle.

 **TOPIC.** The discovery of Tutankhamun's tomb is a modern legend. Ask the class to imagine they were there. On 4 November 1922, Howard Carter, exploring tomb sites in the Valley of the Kings, came into work to find that his digging team had unearthed a carved step in the foundations of houses built for the workforce constructing Ramses VI's tomb. A flight of 16 neat steps emerged by the next day and at the bottom of the staircase, a sealed door. Howard Carter cabled his rich sponsor, Lord Carnarvon, then prowled the site, probably biting his nails down to the elbow, waiting for Lord Carnarvon to travel from England. The two men inspected the door, carefully clearing rocks and rubble. Under trembling fingers, Carter could feel a raised seal. Blowing away the dust of centuries, he stared at something he had dreamt of discovering; the intact seal of Tutankhamun. (This story continues in Valley of the Kings in the next episode!)

 **TOPIC.** Set up a wall-map to study Egypt's trade links. Desert diamonds were certainly found in Egypt, and South Africa's mines are legendary, producing such marvels as the Cullinan diamond, found in Pretoria in 1905 (3106 carats). Opals acquired in Constantinople's markets found their way to Egypt through many merchants' hands. Turquoise came from Sinai, silver vases, ivory dishes and gold perfume bottles from Syria, exotic birds from the land of Punt (now Eritrea) south of Egypt, panthers, cheetahs, leopards and lions from the traders of the Cush, ostrich eggs (poached with honey – a desert dessert?), giraffe tail fly swats, alabaster and marble, furs, feathers and live baboons on leashes from Nubia, plant extracts for medicine, hippo teeth, elephant tusks and incense trees from even deeper in Africa and rich blue lapis lazuli from what is now Afghanistan.

 **ART & CRAFT.** Take this song as inspiration for a painting exhibition. Crushed lapis lazuli made a blue pigment to paint the desert sky on wall friezes in tombs. Green malachite, a copper ore, was powdered, mixed with egg white and gum arabic and used for palm trees, lotus plants and to create the cool green of the Nile. Soot from the base of a cooking pot or scraped from a charred stick made black paint.

THE SONG

 **SING IT.**

SOLO

The desert sky of Egypt,
Is a Pharoah's robe of blue.
And the stars are shards of diamonds
From the mountains of Peru.

The moon's a giant opal
From old Constantinople,
Sending moonbeams down as searchlights,
Guarding Tutankhamun's tomb.

The desert sun of Egypt
Is an orb of Pharoah's gold,
Glowing warmly in the Next World
To prevent him growing old.

The clouds are beds of feathers
To rock him in all weathers,
And the shroud of night, a mantle
To keep him from the cold.

MUSICAL SCORE – page 35

CAIRO KYLE THE CROCODILE

DIRECTOR'S NOTES

A jazzy, foot-tapping number. Impromptu dancing will fill the aisles!

 **SING IT.** Cairo Kyle needs to be able to carry this production number with Miles and Giles supporting their dad.

 **SAY IT.** The 'Snap, snap!' lines can be said with dentist-defying clacks.

 **DRAMA.** Cairo Kyle and the boys can be simply costumed in snazzy waistcoats and jazzy bowties (see front cover).

 **DRAMA.** Beg or borrow real live brass instruments for the lads if you can. Sorry about the sousaphone – please, no hate mail.

 **TOPIC.** Crocodiles did indeed cruise the Nile in ancient times, snacking on sleepy sailors and adventurous children. To quote Lewis Carroll: 'How doth the little crocodile improve his shining tail, and pour the waters of the Nile on every golden scale!' Crocodiles shared the river in those days with hippopotami (Greek for river horse) – hunted by brave men (or lunatics, depending on your standpoint) hurling spears from papyrus boats. Hippo meat was a barbecue favourite at the feast of Osiris.

Hippos, notoriously bad-tempered, were linked with the god of evil, our old pal Seth. Their teeth and tusks were prized ivory, carved into figurines and jewellery. Nile nights echoed to the skin-tingling sounds of crocodiles sliding slinkily through the dark green water, hippos fighting at dusk (clashing those huge teeth) herons calling and, far out in the desert, the Red Land, leopards and lions roaring at the sky as jackals and foxes scuttled quickly past, hunting jerboa (desert mice).

 **ART & CRAFT.** Make and paint a neon sign for the Club Big Bite. Construct cardboard instruments if real brass ones present too much of a nightmare. Start a Nile wildlife wallchart.

 **TOPIC.** Which other creatures would form Cairo Kyle's audience at the Big Bite? Enter stage left, crawling or creeping in from the desert: shy lizards, large monitors, snakes and gazelles, camels and oryx. Enter stage right, from the banks of the Nile: wily water buffalo, wild boar, graceful herons, sacred ibis, gangly storks and white egrets. Swooping in from the high desert sky: ugly vultures, haughty hawks and fierce falcons. Drifting down from the date palms: comically-crested hoopoes, noisy cuckoos, nightingales and green bee-eaters and scuttling in from the sagebush and cacti: spiteful scorpions, sticky-footed geckoes and clever chameleons.

 **FX.** Teeth-snapping bites – clapping!

THE SONG

 **SING IT.**

CAIRO KYLE:
I'm Cairo Kyle the Crocodile,
I'm a lovely guy with a lovely smile.
Lived a lovely life in the lovely Nile,
I'm Cairo Kyle, snap, snap,
The Crocodile.

CAIRO KYLE:
I'm a father to hundreds of crocodiles,
There's Big Boy Miles and Baby Giles.

CAIRO, MILES and GILES:
We're jazzin' jivin' Nile reptiles,
Going out on the town, snap, snap,
For a night on the tiles.

ENSEMBLE:
He's Cairo Kyle the Crocodile,
He's a lovely guy with a lovely smile.
Lived a lovely life in the lovely Nile.

CAIRO KYLE:
I'm Cairo Kyle, snap, snap,
The Crocodile.

CAIRO, MILES and GILES:
We play at a place called Club Big Bite,
Where every night is a Saturday night.

CAIRO KYLE:
I strut my stuff on a slide trombone,
Baby Giles drives 'em wild, snap, snap,
On that old sousaphone.

(DANCE BREAK – 1 CHORUS)

ENSEMBLE:
He's Cairo Kyle the Crocodile,
He's a lovely guy with a lovely smile.
Lived a lovely life in the lovely Nile.

CAIRO KYLE:
I'm Cairo Kyle, snap, snap!

MILES & GILES:
Snap, snap!

CAIRO KYLE:
Snap, snap!
The Crocodile!

MUSICAL SCORE – page 39

SING IT AND SAY IT (FINALE)

DIRECTOR'S NOTES

SING IT. Not a lot of extra work involved here, we promise, because you and your class already know the words for the closing number because it was also the opening number.

DRAMA. The repeat of the last line creates a rousing finish. We suggest a pantomime-style deep bow or similar theatrical flourish at this point before the audience storms the stage for autographs.

TOPIC. Organize your class to write 30 words each, giving their impressions of this **SING IT AND SAY IT** episode. It's a very useful exercise and we always find the results fascinating. If you'd like to pass on their insights and comments to us, we'd be delighted to hear from you – and your class.

THE SONG

SING IT.

ENSEMBLE:
Sing it and say it, can anyone play it?
There's no need to be shy.
Sing it and say it, can anyone play it?
Come on, let's give it a try.

You'll soon learn the tune in a jiff and a half,
You'll soon learn the words, they might make you laugh!
So listen to me, there's no need to read,
Rhyme and rhythm are all you need –

SAY IT.

TEACHER:
Sing it with me on the count of three –
One, two, three . . .

ENSEMBLE: Four!

SING IT.

ENSEMBLE:
Sing it and say it, can anyone play it?
There's no need to be shy.
Sing it and say it, can anyone play it?
Come on, let's give it a,
Let's give it a,
Let's give it a try!

MUSICAL SCORE – page 43

GLOSSARY

RIPPLES   Liquid wrinkles.

ROARS   Ripples in a bad mood.

NUGGETS   Lumps of highly precious metal bearing a striking resemblance to over-sized chunks of breakfast cereal.

PHAROAH   The all-powerful, he (or she)-who-will-not-be-argued-with monarch.

WEALTH   A lot of whatever you desire.

SLAVE   You work hard, day and night. The conditions are terrible. The uniform's awful. The pay's diabolical.

MOULD   A shape to make other shapes, all the same shape.

MELTED   That end-of-summer-term feeling.

SPELLS   Words with the power to change things, always a handy item in a grown-up's arsenal.

ODES   Lilting, lyrical poems in praise of a specific subject or person.

JEWELLER   Someone who makes a beautiful thing from something which was naturally beautiful in the first place.

SCREAM   A violent vocal expression of particularly piercing intensity. Definitely worth practising.

SCOLD   Nagging and needling, nastily.

OVERTIME   Extra work for an excellent rate. (Slaves, teachers and parents are exempt.)

OVERLOAD   You're cooking pancakes for your children, your sister's children and the dog. The phone rings, the cat's sick, two of the children (never yours) are eating raw batter, your son's feeding curry powder to the baby and then someone knocks on the front door. That's overload.

SPLENDOUR   Marvellously magnificent (from the Latin, *splendere*, to shine). How splendiferous.

BATTLES   Playground fights, taken too far.

RAMSES   Sometimes spelt (which is sometimes spelt spelled) Rameses. Egypt was ruled by various Ramses, but we sing about Ramses II who built the Great Temple at Abu Simbel and died in c 1225 BC.

TUTANKHAMUN   Egypt's boy-king of the 18th dynasty who lived from 1361 to 1352 BC.

SETH	God of deserts and storms, a moody deity. Also the name of Adam's third son (Old Testament), sent by God in place of the murdered Abel.
ANCIENT	It's older than ordinary old. But who decides where old ends and ancient starts?
ROBE	A long frock crossed with a full cloak.
SHARDS	Sharp hards.
OPAL	A milky precious stone; an earthbound moon.
CONSTANTINOPLE	Byzantium to the Romans. Istanbul to Turkey's tourists of today (see also **SING IT AND SAY IT, A Bookful of Asia**).
ORB	A sphere of precious metal held in the hand of the monarch on state occasions.
MANTLE	A loose, sleeveless cloak.
CROCODILE	A carnivorous newt on growth hormones.
STRUT	A swaggering stroll.
TROMBONE	It's three metres of straight brass tubing having a bad day. Old English name: sackbut (as in 'How the sackbut do I play this thing?').
SOUSAPHONE	A big brass instrument for a big brave musician.

NILE STYLE

SING IT AND SAY IT

Easily

mf

ENSEMBLE

Sing it and say it, can a-ny-one play it?__ There's no need to be

shy. Sing it and say it, can a-ny-one play it?__ Come on, let's give it a try!

__ You'll soon learn the tune in a jiff and a half, You'll soon learn the words, they

RIVER NILE

-to-ri-a's home, My birth-place, my source, Through the des-ert I flow on a nor-ther-ly course. Through Su-

Ah_____ Ah_____

-dan in-to E-gypt, I broa-den and swell as I glide past the gold mines, Near A-bu Sim-bel.

Ah_____ Ah_____ Ah_____

cresc.

DESERT GOLD

A la 'chain-gang'

SLAVES GROUP 1
SPOKEN

Dig, dig, dig, dig, dig, dig, dig.

SLAVES GROUP 2

We've been

NORTH WITH THE NILE

Still flowing

Far a-

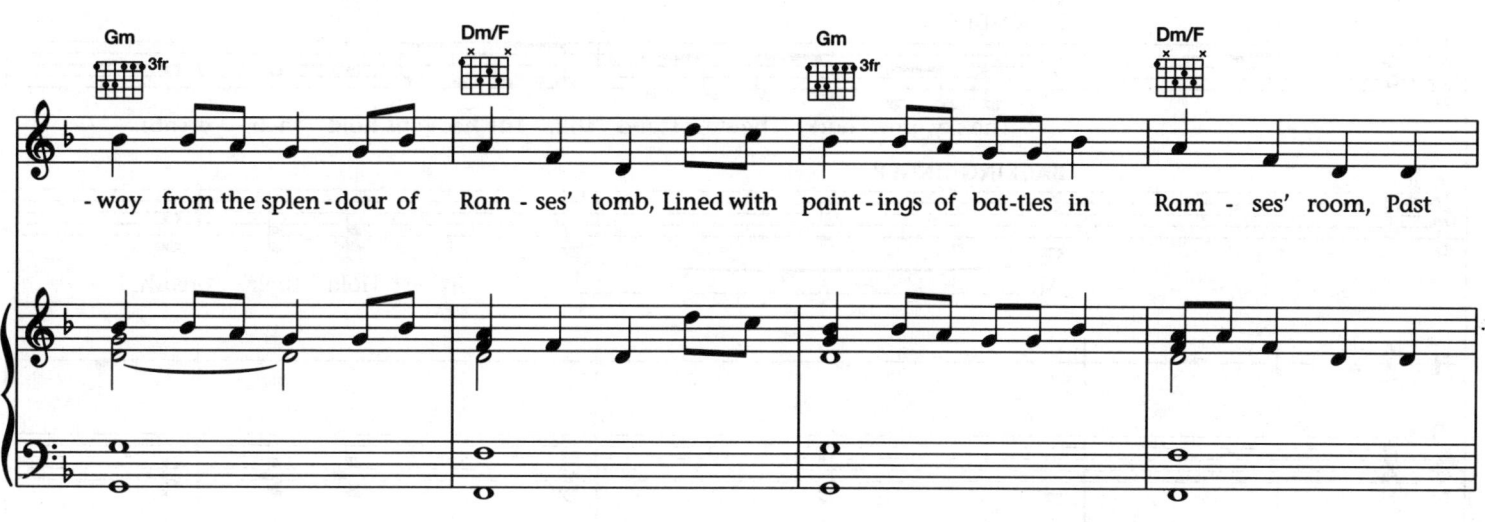

-way from the splen-dour of Ram-ses' tomb, Lined with paint-ings of bat-tles in Ram-ses' room, Past

Lux-or, or Thebes, As the ci-ty was known, To the Val-ley of Kings, Home of Tu-tan-kha-mun.

BACKING SINGERS

Ah_____ Ah_____ Ah Tu-tan-kha-mun.

INTO THE LIGHT

TUTANKHAMUN

AFTERLIFE DREAM

Dreamily of course!

CAIRO KYLE THE CROCODILE

Snappily

CAIRO KYLE

SING IT AND SAY IT (FINALE)

Easily

Sing it and say it, can a-ny-one play it?__ There's no need to be shy.

Sing it and say it, can a-ny-one play it?__ Come on, let's give it a try!__ You'll

soon learn the tune in a jiff and a half, You'll soon learn the words they might make you laugh! So

8va

2   LAND OF THE SUN GOD

CONTENTS

	Director's Notes	Musical Score
SING IT AND SAY IT	46	64
VALLEY OF THE KINGS	48	66
TO KARNAK	50	69
JOURNEY OF THE SUN GOD	52	70
NILE MUD, NILE FLOOD	54	73
BLACK MUD	56	74
CLEOPATRA	58	78
SCRIBBLE IT, SCRIBE	60	80
SING IT AND SAY IT (FINALE)	62	85
GLOSSARY	63	

This **SING AND SAY IT** episode opens with the cautionary tale of doomed tomb bandits in the **VALLEY OF THE KINGS**. Escaping, we glide with the Nile **TO KARNAK** and the temple of Re to witness the **JOURNEY OF THE SUN GOD** as he travels across the heavens. More watery commentary in **NILE MUD, NILE FLOOD**, then we join in the story of the river's annual 'inundation' in **BLACK MUD**. The life and death of Egypt's famous and beautiful queen are told in the haunting **CLEOPATRA** and we meet a band of lively characters in the rapid-fire **SCRIBBLE IT, SCRIBE**. Welcome to the Land of the Sun God!

CAST LIST

SING IT AND SAY IT	**Solo:** teacher, the one in charge (well, almost) **Ensemble:** everybody join in!
VALLEY OF THE KINGS	**Ensemble:** singing a dramatic saga of robbers and curses
TO KARNAK	**Ensemble:** introducing their hero, the majestic River Nile **Solo:** the Nile, leading us to the holy temple of Re
JOURNEY OF THE SUN GOD	**Solo:** High Priest, grandly recounting Re's travels **Ensemble:** in joyful praise of their favourite deity
NILE MUD, NILE FLOOD	**Solo:** the Nile, fluidly feeding us a flow of facts **Backing Singers:** with supportive 'ah'-ing
BLACK MUD	**Ensemble:** in two groups, with cheerful thanks for the Nile's annual gift
CLEOPATRA	**Solo:** engrossing us in the tale of an Egyptian queen **Ensemble:** an eerie echo
SCRIBBLE IT, SCRIBE	**Solo:** a trainee scribe, hieroglyphically challenged! **Ensemble:** a lively group encouraging our hero to 'scratch it on a tablet with a stick'
SING IT AND SAY IT (FINALE)	**Solo:** teacher, the one in charge (well, almost) **Chorus:** everybody join in!

SING IT AND SAY IT

> DIRECTOR'S NOTES

Our first song expresses the essence of the **SING IT AND SAY IT** project:

SING IT.   Singing easy-to-learn music
SAY IT.   Saying entertaining words with rhyme and rhythm
PLAY IT.   Playing simple accompaniments

We'd add **BUILDING** to that list. Building confidence, vocabulary and musical ability. Building concentration and timing, teamwork and, discipline.

The other word which encapsulates **SING IT AND SAY IT** is FUN. Fun in learning *and* fun in teaching.

 **SING IT.**   The first and last sections of this song are identical for easy learning and the whole song is repeated at the end of this 10-minute episode.

 **SING IT.**   **SING IT AND SAY IT** can be performed as an ensemble, in separate groups or as a solo.

 **FX.** Clapping and clicking of fingers will find their natural places in this song.

 **DRAMA.** However you use the material, your class will have plenty of suggestions for actions and simple dance routines. **PLAY IT** may inspire actions like miming a trombone player, pianist or guitarist. Someone will want to conduct the class and everyone will want to shout 'Four!' (after 'One, Two, Three').

 **SAY IT.** Audition for a natural leader to take the part of teacher. Oh, you want to do it? Go on, then.

THE SONG

 **SING IT.**

ENSEMBLE: Sing it and say it, can anyone play it?
There's no need to be shy.
Sing it and say it, can anyone play it?
Come on, let's give it a try.

You'll soon learn the tune in a jiff and a half,
You'll soon learn the words, they might make you laugh!
So listen to me, there's no need to read,
Rhyme and rhythm are all you need –

 **SAY IT.**

TEACHER: Sing it with me on the count of three –
One, two, three . . .

ENSEMBLE: Four!

 **SING IT.**

ENSEMBLE: Sing it and say it, can anyone play it?
There's no need to be shy.
Sing it and say it, can anyone play it?
Come on, let's give it a try.

MUSICAL SCORE – page 64

VALLEY OF THE KINGS

DIRECTOR'S NOTES

A cautionary tale, embalmed (sorry!) in a beautiful song.

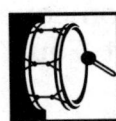 **PLAY IT.** Cymbal, dramatically crashed.

 **DRAMA.** Stage this as a straight-sung song or cast non-speaking roles to mime the action: a sinister snake guard(ess), reputedly the gruesome serpent goddess Meretseger, spitting deadly venom at foolhardy tomb robbers; a monstrous hippo of a security officer with massive teeth (did we say it was going to be easy?) and a 'job's-worth' attitude, recumbent Pharoahs and unrepentant robbers with short futures.

 **TOPIC.** The Valley of the Kings lies in the Western Desert near Thebes, high in the cliffs, safe from the threat of Nile flood damage. All the Pharoahs from Tutmosis I in 1504 BC to Ramses XI in 1070 BC were buried there – totalling over 60 tombs. A former circus strongman, Giovanni Belzone, discovered one of the most magnificent tombs, belonging to Seti I, in 1817. Every centimetre of its 100 metre (328 foot) long walls is covered with exquisite paintings and carvings.

 **TOPIC.** The riches of Tutankhamun's tomb. Howard Carter opened the doors of history in 1922. Ask the class to imagine his feelings. Run a read-aloud story session with their impressions. As his shaking hand pushed a candle into the tomb, hot air, prisoner of centuries, rushed past him. The glint of gold, gold and more gold shone through the swirling dust, gold caskets, gem-studded gold jewellery, and a throne smothered in gold. The second inner coffin, covered in gold. The third coffin, made of solid gold and the pièce de resistance, the mask of Tutankhamun. Alabaster vases, chariots, beds and chairs, all beautifully carved. Weapons for battle in the Next World, musicians buried with their instruments (no Musicians' Union in those days), forty jars of wine, bunches of herbs and flowers, bread, cake and cases of roast duck (no take-aways in the Next World either). Tutankhamun was buried with his childhood toys: model boats, a lock of hair from his gran, Queen Tiye and 413 *shabtis* (or *ushabtis*) – carved wooden figures who would take the night shift for their king if Osiris called him in to work.

 **ART & CRAFT.** Start a wallchart collage of drawings of objects found in the tomb or make clay or papier mâché models, and stage an exhibition in your reception area for parents and friends of the school to visit when they come in for your Egypt-themed assembly.

THE SONG

 **SING IT.**

ENSEMBLE:
Deep in the hills
To the west of the Nile,
Lies a gash in the cliff
Like a dry sandy smile,
Where the Pharoahs of Egypt
Lay buried in style.
In their tombs in the rock
They were safe, for a while,
In the Valley of the Kings.

Protected by spirits,
A serpentine guard
And a huge hippopotamus
Scary and scarred.
The Pharoahs slept soundly,
Awaiting the day
When they would break bread
With the great sun-god, Re,
In the Valley of the Kings.

Then robbers came raiding,
Their hunger for gold
Was disturbing the Pharoahs,
Before they grew cold.
But the spirits were watching,
They would not forgive.
The robbers had riches, but . . .
No time to live!

MUSICAL SCORE – page 66

TO KARNAK

DIRECTOR'S NOTES

A mini-version of our earlier Nile anthem.

 **TOPIC.** Karnak and the Temple of Re. A magnificent monument, taller than a nine-storey building, lined with towering columns topped with carved papyrus heads. The walls are covered with hieroglyphic inscriptions and records of battle victories, and the grounds once had orchards full of fruit trees, beautiful gardens and extensive living quarters for the temple workers. Ask the class to imagine what it must have been like to be a stonemason or an architect on such a project.

 **TOPIC.** The Pharoah would have sailed the river in a sumptuously decorated barge, complete with golden throne, accompanied by his personal advisers. These would have included: the Keeper of the Royal Tombs, the Lord of the Necropolis, the most powerful high priest in the kingdom, skilled cooks preparing delicious banquets of roast goose and hare, and slaves waving feather fans to cool the royal brow.

The Egyptians were the first to make sails and their single-masted, single-sailed vessels (*feluccas*) are still used today on the river. Oars were carried for still days when fishermen might become becalmed and at the mercy of the current or a hungry crocodile. There was little movement on the Nile after dark – the danger of hitting a hidden sandbank was too great. Hunting parties sailed across to islands in the wide parts of the river, using hunting sticks hurled like boomerangs to kill birds, destined for the table.

 **TOPIC.** Rich nobles built villas and farmhouses on the banks of the Nile. What benefits did living by a river offer? Start with water, crops, food, transport and an escape route in times of danger.

From their houses along the waterway, these wealthy men and their families watched the Egyptian sun rise on date palms, groves of silvery olive and green fig trees, and fields full of dainty flax plants with sky-blue flowers, destined to be woven into fine linen. Peasants picked their bunches of ripe purple grapes and rosy pomegranates. Women, with white linen scarves over their hair, did the dusty work of winnowing – throwing wooden trays of newly harvested emmer wheat up into the warm Egyptian breeze, letting the wind blow away the chaff whilst the heavier, more valuable grain, fell to the ground and was saved in papyrus baskets to be milled into flour for the coarse Egyptian bread.

THE SONG

 **SING IT.**

ENSEMBLE

River Nile
River Nile

NILE:

I'll
Tell you how Egypt turns   Ah
Night into day at the   Ah
Temple of Karnak, de-   Ah
-voted to Re.   Ah

MUSICAL SCORE – PAGE 69

JOURNEY OF THE SUN GOD

DIRECTOR'S NOTES

An unusual song explaining the ancient Egyptians' view of time by recounting a day in the life of Re.

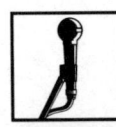 **SING IT.** This can be performed as a **SING IT** or a **CHANT IT**.

 **SAY IT.** The repeated line "Hail, god of the sun" is effective as a **SAY IT**.

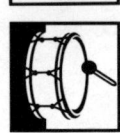 **PLAY IT.** Cymbal, ceremoniously crashed. Borrow a gong and give it a bash!

 **DRAMA.** Hold auditions for a High Priest – an imposing presence. This role, with its commanding character, could do wonders for a child in need of a confidence boost. Costume your High Priest in fine white linen (that old sheet again) and tell your auditioning pupils that priests had shaven heads and four baths a day!

 **DRAMA.** Make your ensemble as large as you like – the more voices, the better. How does the class see the congregation? Kneeling before the priest? Standing in a semi-circle around him? Walking towards him in pairs chanting their response line? Put it to the vote – or use their original ideas.

 **ART & CRAFT.** Form a design team for a *Journey of the Sun God* collage. Re is seen as a man with a sun and serpent on top of his hawk's head. His dawn to dawn trip across the sky represents the Pharoah's procession along the Nile. Paint Re's sacred solar boat and gold sun disc. The boat is often decorated with swallows, heralding dawn and the changing seasons. A falcon or hawk is another favourite adornment, shown descending from the sky, representing the sun's rays flying to earth under the protection of the hawk-god, Horus.

Detail Re's night-long journey through the Underworld. Anubis, god of the dead, spent time down there. A jackal-headed fellow, his job spec was to weigh the heart of the dead to see if the deceased was pure enough to enter the Next World. Osiris, Lord of the Underworld, sported a fetching crown of reeds and ostrich feathers, and carried a crook and flail to prove he was a king. For a different slant on the Underworld, see **SING IT AND SAY IT, A Bookful of Ancient Greece** for our contemporary version of the story of Hades and Persephone.

 **TOPIC.** Re the family man. His children Tefnut (god of rain) and Shu (god of air) were parents of Geb (god of the earth) and Nut (god of the sky). Their children were Osiris, his wife Isis, stormy old Seth and his wife Nephthys. Re was also father of all the stars in the heavens. Another of Re's children was Bastet, the cat-headed goddess of love. All cats were sacred to her and much revered. When a family cat died, the whole household shaved off their eyebrows! Hundreds of mummified cats were buried at Bastet's temple in the Nile delta. She also controlled the power of the sun to ripen crops, gaining her a strong following amongst farming folk!

THE SONG

 **SING IT.**

ENSEMBLE: Ah, ah, ah, ah, ah

HIGH PRIEST: Pray to Re for the dawning day,
ENSEMBLE: Hail, god of the sun.

HIGH PRIEST: Dawning day as he sails away,
ENSEMBLE: Hail, god of the sun.

HIGH PRIEST: Sails away in his sacred boat,
ENSEMBLE: Hail, god of the sun.

HIGH PRIEST: Sacred boat in the sky afloat,
ENSEMBLE: Hail, god of the sun.

HIGH PRIEST: He banishes cold with his disc of gold,
ENSEMBLE: Hail, god of the sun.

HIGH PRIEST: Disc of gold through the heavens rolled,
ENSEMBLE: Hail, god of the sun.

HIGH PRIEST: Rolled all night through the Underworld,
ENSEMBLE: Hail, god of the sun.

HIGH PRIEST: The Underworld where the dawn unfurled,
ENSEMBLE: Hail, god of the sun.

MUSICAL SCORE – page 70

NILE MUD, NILE FLOOD

DIRECTOR'S NOTES

More Nile facts – set to a tune you are all beginning to know so well!

TOPIC. The waters of the Nile were (and are) totally essential to the well-being of Egypt with its thousands of miles of arid desert. Various means of irrigation were practised, some of which are still in use today. The *shaduf*, a counter-balanced scoop or bucket on a long swivelling pole, was often worked by two men. The *tanbur*, or Archimedes' Screw (see **SING IT AND SAY IT, A Bookful of Ancient Greece**) was simple, widespread and very effective. Waterwheels turned by camel, human, ox or donkey tipped valuable H_2O into channels to feed fields of flax, wheat and barley. When the Nile, topped up by melted snow feeding down from Africa's mountains, brought its life-giving gift of flood, farmers trapped water behind lagoons and mudbanks and used it to bring relief to wilting lettuces, onions, beans, melons and cucumbers parching under the hot Egyptian sun!

ART & CRAFT. Build simple working models of water-extraction equipment. Ask a craft-minded Mum or Dad to come in and work with your class.

TOPIC. Damming the Nile – for and against. Set up debating teams. The first dam was built in 1842, north of Cairo, across the delta. The Aswan Dam was constructed between 1899 and 1902, during which period of history Kitchener and his British troops were fighting the Boer War further south in Africa. The High Dam, President Nasser's 1960's dream, increased agricultural land in Egypt by 2% – it's only 94% desert these days! So, the Nile no longer floods: crops are harvested twice a year, hydroelectricity has arrived, tourists visit the dams and more land has been snatched back from the Sahara. At what price? The people of Lower Nubia, proud farmers of their lands since Biblical times, had to be resettled when their homes vanished under water. The cleansing power of the yearly flood has been removed, resulting in increased salt levels in the soil – and plants don't like saline. Drainage systems are being built instead of irrigation ditches, to drain away sour water. Salt is also partly responsible for the erosion of Egypt's ancient monuments, eating away her heritage. Should be a lively discussion!

TOPIC. Set up a small crop project. Grow mustard and cress or 'sprouters' like runner, broad or mung beans, or alfalfa. Run experiments with seeds in different conditions: bone-dry as they would be in the desert, damp (on blotting paper), wet (in standing water) and in salt water to see how they compare. Elect a team of scientists and lab technicians to monitor progress daily and report to the rest of the class. Appoint team artists to draw progress sketches. Then sell your crop to the school canteen. Only joking!

THE SONG

 **SING IT.**

NILE: My water is borrowed
         By ditch or shaduf.
         My mud makes a brick
         For a wall or a roof.   BACKING SINGERS
         The
         Mountains of Africa   Ah
         Feed me all year, by Ju-   Ah
         -ly I'm in flood,   Ah
         Hear the farmers all cheer.

MUSICAL SCORE – page 73

BLACK MUD

DIRECTOR'S NOTES

A lively song with the flavour of a spiritual.

 **SING IT.** Recruit (or press-gang) as many of your class as you can for this rousing ensemble number. Why not use the whole school?

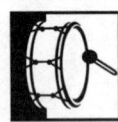 **PLAY IT.** An unusual melody with unexpected chromatic notes.

 **FX.** Clapping – and persuade the audience to join in.

 **DRAMA.** Dress your farmers, their wives and children in pure white linen (well, alright, polyester cotton. Yes, time to raid the airing cupboard again – tablecloths, sheets and pillowcases to the fore), bare feet (cheap costuming) and wigs – see below.

 **ART & CRAFT.** Make a range of Egyptian wigs (big fringe, shoulder length hair) from black wool stitched to a simple fabric skullcap. Let each member of the class design his or her own headband or opt for the white cotton scarf as protection against the sun.

 **TOPIC.** The Nile flood. Every year the African sun melted the snow on the mountains of the Ethiopian Highlands and fed the Blue and White Niles. An enormous volume of water pushed into Egypt and in July or early August the Nile burst its banks and flooded an area the size of England, depositing a thick layer of rich black silt and forming the blessed Black Land (*kemet*). This fertile soil was seeded as soon as the waters started to recede. Sheep were herded over the land, treading in the seed. The farmers then sat back and waited for high-quality crops to sprout. Food was eaten fresh, stored, pickled, dried or preserved in oil and was used to trade or barter for other goods.

 **TOPIC.** Egypt's seasons. July to October was the Time of Inundation when many farmers went to work on the pyramids whilst the flood fed their fields. November to February was the Time of Emergence when crops were sown to the sound of magical spells and musical chants and grew swiftly in warm, wet conditions. March to June was the Time of Harvest – quick, get the crops in before the Nile floods again! Everyone helped, even the priests. Sickles flashed in the sun – no combine harvesters then. Musicians played celebratory songs and anthems. Enormous harvest suppers fed hungry workers as dusk fell.

 **TOPIC.** Papyrus. A member of the same family as sedge grass and bulrushes, papyrus is a marsh plant which grew in profusion along the Nile. It was harvested and taken to riverside workshops where its solid triangular stem was cut into short lengths, peeled and sliced into strips. To make paper, the strips were placed side by side, one layer vertically, the next horizontally. Cloths and weights were placed over it, allowing the natural juices to glue the layers together. The paper was polished with a stone and must have been fascinating to write on. Papyrus was also used for ropes, sandals, mats, boxes, chests, baskets, sieves and, as we say in the song, boats and fishing nets.

THE SONG

 **SING IT.**

ENSEMBLE:

Hey, River Nile,
How about it?
Are you ready
for the great Nile flood?
Hey, River Nile,
How about it?
'Cause we're ready
for that black, black Nile mud.

Black mud is the colour of life on the Nile,
Black mud means the people won't starve on the Nile.
Black mud means the people can smile, smile, smile
And give thanks to the god of the River Nile.

Give thanks for the emmer wheat for our bread,
Give thanks for the linen flax for our thread,
Give thanks for the grapes for a fine wine
And give thanks for the sun and its sunshine.

Hey, River Nile,
How about it?
Are you ready
for the great Nile flood?
Hey, River Nile,
How about it?
'Cause we're ready
for that black, black Nile mud.

Black mud means a farmer can farm on the Nile,
Black mud means a family can thrive on the Nile.
Black mud means the people can smile, smile, smile
And give thanks to the god of the River Nile.

Give thanks for papyrus for paper boats,
Give thanks for papyrus for paper notes.
Give thanks for papyrus for fishing nets
And give thanks for the fish as the sun sets.

GROUPS 1 and 2:

Hey, River Nile,
How about it?
Are you ready
for the great Nile flood?
Hey, River Nile,
How about it?
'Cause we're ready
for that black, black Nile mud.

MUSICAL SCORE – page 74

CLEOPATRA

| DIRECTOR'S NOTES |

A haunting song with a melody to linger in your memory.

SING IT. Two simple, but very important singing roles for a solo and an ensemble for an atmosphere-building echo. Add hissing for extra sibilance on 'shake' in the last line.

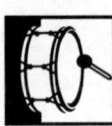

PLAY IT. Triangle, regally played.

TOPIC. Caesar and Cleopatra. Now, Cleo was by most accounts a beautiful woman, although several historians insist that her nose was enormous! The French poet, Blaise Pascal, wrote in the 1600's: "Had Cleopatra's nose been shorter, the whole face of the world would have changed." Who knows? (sorry). She was reputedly a skilled linguist and a witty lady who resorted to bribery, blackmail and downright deviousness as the need arose – the deaths of two of her brothers, a sister and an Armenian king are attributed to her.

Caesar met Cleopatra in 48 BC when he was 54 and she was 21 (see also **Cleopatra, Pamper Me, Please in SING IT AND SAY IT, A Bookful of Ancient Rome**). She was married to her brother at the time and he, on reaching the age of 14, had snatched the throne from her and proclaimed himself King Ptolemy XIV. Caesar sided with Cleopatra and restored her to queenship. She later accompanied the Dictator of Rome home. Roman society took great umbrage at her arrival. Caesar's plan to marry her, take the title of King of Egypt and move the capital of the Roman Empire to Alexandria was as popular with Rome's elders as Nero and a box of matches. Beware the Ides of March, indeed.

TOPIC. Cleopatra and Mark Antony. History suggests that Cleopatra sailed to Syria at the invitation of one of Rome's clever generals, Mark Antony, a man loyal to the memory of Caesar. She apparently glided into harbour on a luxurious gold-plated barge complete with billowing purple sails and a sumptuous dinner at the ready (must have had a microwave in the galley). Mark Antony, accustomed to army food, didn't hesitate to accept her invitation to dine.

He and Cleopatra parted for three years during their relationship but when they met up again, he presented her with a gift – Cyprus. Then he added chunks of Syria, Phoenicia and Judea. Was she satisfied? She was not. She asked for more Syria, but a certain King Herod owned it at the time. Mark Antony gave her the Gardens of Jericho instead.

In later years, on hearing that Cleopatra was dead, Mark Antony threw himself on his sword in grief, but hadn't quite departed this earth when in walked Cleo. Typical, he thought – and died. The lady ran an asses' milk bath, thought about it for a while (for months, some said) then did the dirty deed with the asp.

THE SONG

 **SING IT.**

SOLO: Cleopatra,
Queen of Egypt.

ENSEMBLE: Cleopatra,
Queen of Egypt.

SOLO: Bathed in milk
ENSEMBLE: From an ass

SOLO: Pretty, pretty Cleopatra.
ENSEMBLE: Pretty, pretty Cleopatra.

SOLO: Lost her life
ALL: To a snake!

MUSICAL SCORE – page 78

SCRIBBLE IT, SCRIBE

| DIRECTOR'S NOTES |

A bouncy, busy number with lots of words – and lots of humour.

SAY IT.   The scribe's part can be a **SAY IT**. If your scribe finds it tricky to sing, let him or her talk it through, almost as a rap. Breathing through the ears helps – it's a tongue-twister!

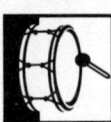

PLAY IT.   Whistles and hooters or any other 'cheeky' musical sounds!

DRAMA.   See front cover for costume ideas, like the 'L' plate. They didn't really wear 'L' plates – we just made that up. What type of person is our scribe? Streetwise? Bewildered? Over-confident? Does he enjoy his work? Read the words with the class and see who they would elect to take the part.

TOPIC.   Hieroglyphics (Greek for 'sacred writing in stone') – 700 difficult, detailed miniature drawings, deliberately kept complex so that few people could learn them, ensuring jobs for the scribes! Devious, hmm? Mind you, it took ten years to memorise the full set. A famous tale concerns the Rosetta Stone, discovered in the Nile delta in 1799 by Jean-François Champollion. At the time, nobody had understood these word pictures for 1600 years because when the Romans took over Egypt in AD 324, hieroglyphics were banned. The stone, a thank you to Cleopatra's relation, Ptolemy V, from his priests, had three sections of script – hieroglyphics, their shorthand version, (demotic) and Greek. Reading the Greek deciphered the hieroglyphics, opening another door on ancient Egypt.

ART & CRAFT.   Draw (or is it write?) hieroglyphics. The sign for A is a hawk, B resembles a boot, L is a lion and M, an owl. Investigate other alphabets: Cuneiform (used 5000 years ago in Mesopotamia before the days of paper – symbols to represent sounds were impressed into damp clay using a wedge-shaped pen), Arabic, Chinese and Greek (see our song **Gamma Rays and River Deltas** in **SING IT AND SAY IT, A Bookful of Ancient Greece**).

TOPIC.   Tax collecting – an old idea that won't lay down and die. Scribes did stock-takes on farms to decide how much was owed to the king. Farmers moved boundary stones to pretend they had smaller fields. Non-payment was a bad idea. In the tomb of Mereruka is a mural – a panel of tax assessors watching villagers grovel with excuses about faulty tax returns. Punishment? A beating – at least. Now, where's that Inland Revenue envelope?

TOPIC.   Scribes had lessons in maths (see, it isn't a new form of torture!) astronomy, astrology, arts, games, sport, politics and social etiquette. A scribe was a writer, clerk, manager, record-keeper, taxman, tutor, government official, seer and sage – rolled into one.

THE SONG

 **SING IT.**

SCRIBE:

I'm a scribe, a trainee academic,
Learning letters, very alphabetic,
Seven hundred tricky hieroglyphics,
Scratch it on a tablet with a stick.

Learning numbers, learning mathematics,
Signs and symbols, very scientific,
Squares and angles, very geometric,
Scratch it on a tablet with a stick.

ENSEMBLE:

Scribble it, scribe, write it down,
Describe, denote, delete it.
Scribble it, scribe, write it down,
Record, recount, receipt it.
Scribble it, scribe, write it down,
Important information.
Scribble it, scribe, write it down,
The history of our nation.

SCRIBE:

Pharoah sends me out to be his taxman,
Farmers hate me, treat me like the axeman,
Counting cattle, got to have the facts man,
Scratch it on a tablet with a stick.

Myths and legends, someone's got to write 'em,
Wars and battles, someone's got to fight 'em,
Scribes stay home and write 'em as an item,
Scratch it on a tablet with a stick.

ENSEMBLE:

Scribble it, scribe, write it down,
Describe, denote, delete it.
Scribble it, scribe, write it down,
Record, recount, receipt it.
Scribble it, scribe, write it down,
Important information.
Scribble it, scribe, write it down,
The history of our nation.

ENSEMBLE:

The history of our	SCRIBE
na-	Note it, jot it,
-tion	Memorise and learn it,
	Scratch it on a tablet
On a tablet	
	With a stick!

MUSICAL SCORE – page 80

SING IT AND SAY IT (FINALE)

DIRECTOR'S NOTES

SING IT.   Not a lot of extra work involved here, we promise, because you and your class already know the words for the closing number because it was also the opening number.

DRAMA.   The repeat of the last line creates a rousing finish. We suggest a pantomime-style deep bow or similar theatrical flourish at this point before the audience storms the stage for autographs.

TOPIC.   Organize your class to write 30 words each, giving their impressions of this **SING IT AND SAY IT** episode. It's a very useful exercise and we always find the results fascinating. If you'd like to pass on their insights and comments to us, we'd be delighted to hear from you – and your class.

THE SONG

SING IT.

ENSEMBLE: Sing it and say it, can anyone play it?
There's no need to be shy.
Sing it and say it, can anyone play it?
Come on, let's give it a try.

You'll soon learn the tune in a jiff and a half,
You'll soon learn the words, they might make you laugh!
So listen to me, there's no need to read,
Rhyme and rhythm are all you need –

SAY IT.

TEACHER: Sing it with me on the count of three –
One, two, three . . .

ENSEMBLE: Four!

SING IT.

ENSEMBLE: Sing it and say it, can anyone play it?
There's no need to be shy.
Sing it and say it, can anyone play it?
Come on, let's give it a,
Let's give it a,
Let's give it a try!

MUSICAL SCORE – page 85

GLOSSARY

DRY	Scratchy and dusty, like your throat by the end of Friday.
TOMBS	Places to bury the dead. Does anyone bury the living?
PROTECTED	Cared for, looked after and generally, um – protected.
SPIRITS	Ethereal beings, usually invisible to the naked eye – unless you've been at the spirits.
SERPENTINE	The late-entry method for Assembly.
HIPPOPOTAMUS	How you feel when you've just had second helpings of steamed treacle pudding with extra custard.
SCARY	Fearsome and frightening – like Day 1 as a teacher.
SCARRED	Boy's knee, aged 7.
RAIDING	Robbing – with attitude.
HUNGER	Yearning with a greedy streak.
RICHES	Not too much of a good thing.
PRAY	Asking nicely for divine favours.
SACRED	Sunday mornings.
UNDERWORLD	A place of deep dark deeds inhabited by creepy, scary creatures. Our loft's a bit like that.
UNFURLED	Curled up, in reverse.
SHADUF	Bucket on a stick.
MUD	Earth, liquidised.
STARVE	Hunger to the power of ten.
SMILE	Rehearsal for a laugh.
FLAX	A delicate plant, usually about 45 cm (18 inches) tall with pretty, cup-shaped blue or red flowers which, quite suddenly, turns into linen.
FARMER	Outdoor optimist.
THRIVE	Survive prosperously.
ASS	Milking one of these for Cleopatra's bath must have been about as popular as cleaning her bath afterwards.
SNAKE	Slithery and devious with a vicious bite and a habit of swallowing food whole. Could be a job spec for an MP.
SCRIBE	From mathematics to music, mythology to medicine, he's your oracle.
TRAINEE	An expert, just starting out.
ACADEMIC	An expert, arrived.
MATHEMATICS	The language of log.
SYMBOLS	Scientific shorthand.
SCIENTIFIC	Systematic study and logical conclusions.
GEOMETRIC	Pythagoras' pension plan.
TAXMAN	He who never giveth it in the first place, but definitely hath the power to taketh it away.
AXEMAN	Similar to the taxman, but differently armed.
MYTHS	Embellished rumours based on honest hearsay.
JOT	Note down – at Formula 1 speed.

LAND OF THE SUN GOD

SING IT AND SAY IT

Easily

Sing it and say it, can a-ny-one play it?_ There's no need to be shy.

Sing it and say it, can a-ny-one play it?_ Come on, let's give it a try!

You'll soon learn the tune in a jiff and a half, You'll soon learn the words, they

VALLEY OF THE KINGS

Wide tempo

CYMBAL (crashed)

ENSEMBLE

Deep in the hills to the west of the Nile, Lies a gash in the cliff Like a dry san-dy smile, Where the

Pha-roahs of E - gypt Lay bur - ied in style. In their tombs in the rock they were safe,

___ for a while, ___ In the Val - ley of the

Then rob - bers came raid - ing, Their

hun - ger for gold Was dis - turb - ing the Pha-roahs Be - fore they grew cold. But the spi - rits were watch-ing, They

would not for-give. The rob - bers had ri - ches but . . . No time to

live!

TO KARNAK

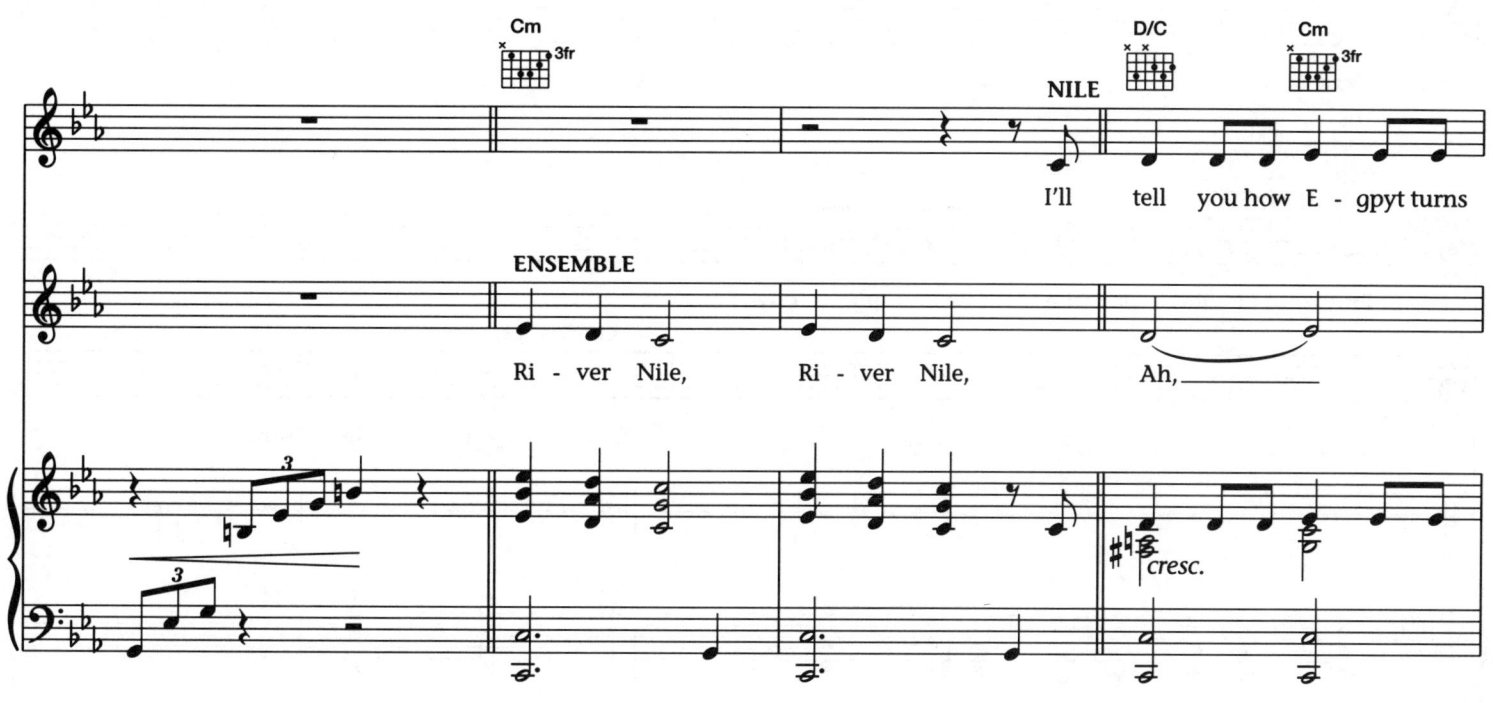

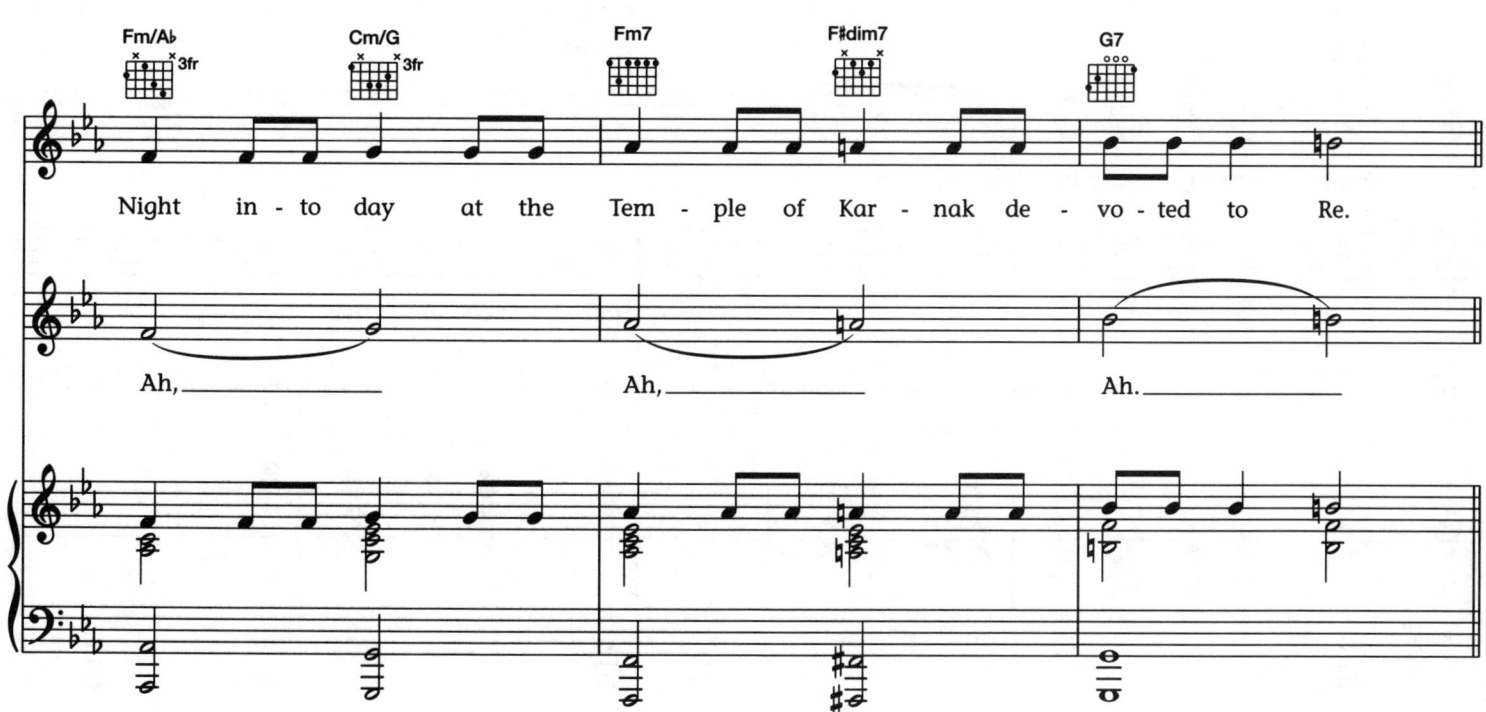

JOURNEY OF THE SUN GOD

Religiously

NILE MUD, NILE FLOOD

Still flowing

NILE

My

wa - ter is bor-row'd by ditch or sha-duf. My mud makes a brick for a wall or a roof. The

moun-tains of Af - ri - ca feed me all year, By Ju - ly I'm in flood, Hear the far-mers all cheer.

BACKING SINGERS

Ah_____ Ah_____ Ah_____

BLACK MUD

Sticky tempo

Hey, Ri - ver Nile, How a - bout it?

Are you rea - dy for the great Nile flood? Hey, Ri - ver Nile, How a - bout it? 'Cause we're

rea - dy for that black, black Nile mud. Black

mud is the col - our of life on the Nile, Black mud means the peo - ple won't starve on the Nile. Black

Are your rea-dy for the great Nile flood? Hey, Ri - ver Nile,

Are you rea-dy for the great Nile flood? Hey, Ri - ver Nile,

How a-bout it? 'Cause we're rea-dy for that black, black Nile mud!

How a-bout it? 'Cause we're rea-dy for that black, black Nile mud!

CLEOPATRA

Gently

SOLO

Cle - o - pa - tra, Queen of E - gypt.

TRIANGLE

SCRIBBLE IT, SCRIBE

Scribbly tempo – fast!

STEMS UP – WHISTLE

STEMS DOWN – HOOTER

SCRIBE

I'm a scribe, a train-ee ac-a-dem-ic, Learn-ing let-ters, ve-ry al-pha-be-tic,

Se-ven hun-dred tri-cky hie-ro-gly-phics, Scratch it on a tab-let with a stick.

Learn-ing num-bers, learn-ing math-e-ma-tics, Signs and sym-bols, ve-ry sci-en-ti-fic,

SING IT AND SAY IT

3   THE PYRAMID FILE
CONTENTS

	Director's Notes	Musical Score
SING IT AND SAY IT	88	103
RIVER NILE TO GIZA	90	105
SANDY SYD THE PYRAMID	92	106
ONE HUNGRY MUMMY	94	110
JINXED SPHINX!	96	114
THE PYRAMID STOP	98	121
SING IT AND SAY IT (FINALE)	100	126
GLOSSARY	102	

In this **SING IT AND SAY IT** episode, we travel along the **RIVER NILE TO GIZA** to meet **SANDY SYD THE PYRAMID**, a lonely little fellow who simply yearns to be tall. **ONE HUNGRY MUMMY** shares her diet secrets with us, then it's the turn of the **JINXED SPHINX** to tell us his life story. We find ourselves amidst a slaves' rebellion in **THE PYRAMID STOP**, rock 'n' rolling us to the end of our travels in ancient Egypt.

CAST LIST

SING IT AND SAY IT	**Solo:** teacher, the one in charge (well, almost) **Ensemble:** everybody join in!
RIVER NILE TO GIZA	**Ensemble:** with the low-down on Egypt's great river **Solo:** the Nile, introducing us to pyramid country
SANDY SYD THE PYRAMID	**Solo:** Sandy Syd, a vertically-challenged pyramid **Ensemble:** tall motherly pyramids
ONE HUNGRY MUMMY	**Solo:** saggily bandaged mummy, once glamorous, now ravenous **Ensemble:** with endless menu ideas for our hungry heroine
JINXED SPHINX!	**Solo:** Sphinx, hoping for sympathy for his lack of a nose **Ensemble:** pyramids who've spent 4000 years listening to the Sphinx going on – and on – and on . . .
THE PYRAMID STOP	**Ensemble:** slaves, hauling blocks, chain-gang style **Solo:** slave leader, the militant influence **Solo:** overseer, resorting to rock 'n' roll to motivate his gang
SING IT AND SAY IT (FINALE)	**Solo:** teacher, the one in charge (well, almost) **Chorus:** everybody join in!

SING IT AND SAY IT

DIRECTOR'S NOTES

Our first song expresses the essence of the **SING IT AND SAY IT** project:

SING IT.   Singing easy-to-learn music
SAY IT.   Saying entertaining words with rhyme and rhythm
PLAY IT.   Playing simple accompaniments

We'd add **BUILDING** to that list. Building confidence, vocabulary and musical ability. Building concentration and timing, teamwork and, discipline.

The other word which encapsulates **SING IT AND SAY IT** is FUN. Fun in learning *and* fun in teaching.

 **SING IT.**   The first and last sections of this song are identical for easy learning and, the whole song is repeated at the end of this 10-minute episode.

 **SING IT.   SING IT AND SAY IT** can be performed as an ensemble, in separate groups or as a solo.

 **FX.**   Clapping and clicking of fingers will find their natural places in this song.

 **DRAMA.**   However you use the material, your class will have plenty of suggestions for actions and simple dance routines. **PLAY IT** may inspire actions like miming a trombone player, pianist or guitarist. Someone will want to conduct the class and everyone will want to shout 'Four!' (after 'One, Two, Three').

 **SAY IT.**   Audition for a natural leader to take the part of teacher. Oh, you want to do it? Go on, then.

THE SONG

 **SING IT.**

ENSEMBLE: Sing it and say it, can anyone play it?
There's no need to be shy.
Sing it and say it, can anyone play it?
Come on, let's give it a try.

You'll soon learn the tune in a jiff and a half,
You'll soon learn the words, they might make you laugh!
So listen to me, there's no need to read,
Rhyme and rhythm are all you need –

 **SAY IT.**

TEACHER: Sing it with me on the count of three –
One, two, three . . .

ENSEMBLE: Four!

 **SING IT.**

ENSEMBLE: Sing it and say it, can anyone play it?
There's no need to be shy.
Sing it and say it, can anyone play it?
Come on, let's give it a try.

MUSICAL SCORE – page 103

RIVER NILE TO GIZA

DIRECTOR'S NOTES

Here's that ole' River Nile, flowing past Memphis to the land of the pyramids.

TOPIC. The search for the Nile's source fired the world's imagination for centuries – like the space race. Scotsman James Bruce thought he'd found it in 1770 (sorry Jim, wrong river). He was followed by Richard Francis Burton (did he stay on to film *Cleopatra*?) and John Hanning Speke. These two had adventures all over Africa, but the mystery remained. Dr David Livingstone continued the search in 1865 and after his death, Henry Stanley took up the challenge and Lake Victoria was declared as X marks the spot.

TOPIC. The wonders of ancient Egypt have been observed from the Nile, Egypt's liquid motorway without roadworks, by various dignatories in a selection of boats. Papyrus craft inspired Thor Heyerdahl to make his Ra expedition. He sailed the oceans, not to prove that ancient Egyptians did, but to prove that they could have. Napoleon chose elegant *dahaibiyyas* for his Nile travels. Lord Kitchener commandeered wooden paddle-steamers, full of pyramid-spotting Victorian tourists on Thomas Cook's original package holidays, to lead his force to avenge the killing of General Gordon.

ART & CRAFT. Make clay or cardboard models of "pyramids tall and pyramids small" and set them in a sand tray with a painted backdrop of the desert sky.

TOPIC. The Great Pyramid of Cheops possess awesome statistics. As tall as a 40-storey building, its base covers 13 acres (5.4 hectares) of land (compare that to an area local to you) – about seven blocks in an American city. It took more stone to build this one pyramid than all England's churches and its original limestone outer coating was 2.4 metres (8 feet) thick. Pliny, the Roman historian (for more on him, see **(SING IT AND SAY IT, A Bookful of Ancient Rome)**, tells of young Egyptians sliding down the pyramid's sides. Fair enough – no banisters.

TOPIC. Saqqara. Standing on a dust-dry plateau, Saqqara is dominated by the Step Pyramid, part of the necropolis built in 2686 BC for King Zoser by the innovative architect, Imhotep. King Zoser was the first king of the 3rd Dynasty whose reign marked the start of the "Pyramid Age" or Old Kingdom. The Step Pyramid started as a flat burial chamber, but Imhotep experimented and added. One purpose of the steps was to enable the king to climb up and enter the Next World by joining the sun-god Re as he entered the heavens at dawn. Egyptologists believe that many more layers of tombs and treasure hide beneath the desert sand. Exciting excavations expected!

THE SONG

 **SING IT.**

ENSEMBLE: River Nile,
River Nile,
From his source
On a course
Of over four thousand miles.
He ripples and roars
And then he rests for a while,
He's a river with style,
The Great River Nile.

NILE:		BACKING SINGERS
	I flow past Saqqara,	
	Where old Imhotep	
	Built King Zoser's pyramid	BACKING SINGERS
	Step by step and	
	On into Giza, where	Ah
	Pyramids tall stand	Ah
	Grand in the sand over	Ah
	Pyramids small.	Ah

MUSICAL SCORE – page 105

SANDY SYD THE PYRAMID

DIRECTOR'S NOTES

A fun number with a great 'Aaah!' factor.

 **SING IT.** Sandy Syd has quite a large part but it isn't too complex. The six pyramids looking down on him have one line each – and those can be **SAY ITS**.

 **DRAMA.** The music has a message of movement in it for "pyramid". Listen to the tape and see if your hands automatically point upwards to meet at a pinnacle!

 **PLAY IT.** Triangle, pyramidically played.

 **DRAMA.** Cast a Sandy Syd with snuffling ability who can summon up a trembling lower lip at will. You see, he believes the builders only constructed him as an afterthought, probably in their tea-break using odd bits of left-over stone. Aaah, bless him. The older pyramids have an auntie-like approach to the poor little fellow.

 **TOPIC.** Pyramids were built with the four sides facing north, south, east and west. Although the ancient Egyptians had no compasses, they read the heavens and were excellent mathematicians and scientists. Their calculations were so accurate that when Sir William Flinders Petrie, known as the father of modern archaeology, measured the Great Pyramid, he found discrepancies of mere centimetres in its dimensions.

Egyptologist Robert Bauval claimed that the Giza pyramids were laid out to mirror the skies, copying the positions of the stars in the belt of Orion. Others believed that the pyramids were early space observatories, backed up by the fact that Cheops' pyramid has four narrow shafts leading from the burial chamber: one points directly to the northern stars which never disappear below the horizon, one points to Orion which the Egyptians believed was the god Osiris shining in the sky, and one of the queen's chamber shafts points to Sirius, thought to be the heavenly body of the goddess, Isis. Was the pyramid designed to navigate Pharoah's journey to the skies? In 1994, scientists sent a tiny robot camera along the narrow southern shaft of the queen's chamber in an attempt to unravel this intriguing mystery. After 60 metres, it was stopped by a small slab of stone with copper handles. What lies behind this miniature door? No one knows – yet. Investigations continue, using microscopic camera equipment.

 **ART & CRAFT.** Draw large and small pyramids to get to grips with three-dimensional ideas, scale and perspective.

THE SONG

SAY IT.

SANDY SYD:	I'm Sandy Syd the Pyramid.
PYRAMIDS:	He's a lonely little pyramid.
SANDY SYD:	They built me the same As they built them all, But they didn't build me big, They built me small.
SANDY SYD: PYRAMID 1:	It's my dream. Oh, he's dreaming every day.
SANDY SYD: PYRAMID 2:	To be tall, Oh, he'd love to be tall.
SANDY SYD: PYRAMID 3:	Looking down Oh, I wish he'd grow up.
SANDY SYD: PYRAMID 4:	On them all. He's always going on about this.
SANDY SYD: PYRAMID 5:	Why, oh why It's a shame, don't you agree?
SANDY SYD: PYRAMID 6:	Can't I be tall? Wait for it . . . it's not fair.
SANDY SYD:	It's not fair, They built me small.
PYRAMIDS:	He's Sandy Syd the Pyramid.
SANDY SYD:	I'm a lonely little pyramid.
PYRAMIDS:	They built him the same As they built us all, But they didn't build him big,
SANDY SYD:	They built me small!

MUSICAL SCORE – PAGE 106

ONE HUNGRY MUMMY

DIRECTOR'S NOTES

A highly dramatic Broadway-style opening to this song introduces us to a formidable 5000 year-old lady!

 **SING IT.** The mummy needs a strong voice to cope with her opening solo and quick-fire lines later in the song. Choose four capable soloists with a good sense of timing and give them four lines each. The fact that the food items are in numerical and alphabetical (almost) order should help with memorising.

 **SAY IT.** The mummy's final line about indigestion is a **SAY IT** – or a **GROAN IT**!

 **PLAY IT.** Cymbal, hungrily crashed.

 **DRAMA.** This mummy was once a glamorous character, possibly an early Egyptian film star, complete with darkly kohled eyes and malachite-green eye shadow. She was famous for her chic appearance, but her bandages, such a fashion statement 5000 years ago, are now looking both dated and tatty. Her figure is in ruins and hunger beckons . . .

 **ART & CRAFT.** Far be it from us to suggest that you use real food for the mummy's first snack in centuries. A papier mâché or cardboard running buffet is both cheaper and safer – and less likely to get you the sack. See front cover for inspirations.

 **TOPIC.** Preservation of mummies. The name comes from the original efforts at mummification which left the body black and, by all accounts, sufficiently brittle that bits snapped off! These black bodies looked like tar or bitumen, and the Arabic word for bitumen is *mummiya* – hence mummy.

THE SONG

 **SING IT.**

MUMMY: For five thousand years I've been soundly asleep,
In a pyramid tomb in a coma so deep.
Not a drop did I drink, not a bite did I eat,
Now my bandages sag, I can see my feet.

I have nothing to wear, I'm so painfully thin,
I've lost all my curves and I'm down to one chin.
Hear that rumbling, grumbling roar in my tum?
Bring me food, bring me food,
This is one hungry mum – my!

I'd like an apple and two bananas,
Three chilli and cheese con carnes,
Four dates from Iran,
Five eggs in a pan,
Six figs in a flan.

SOLO 1: (*shouted*) And a gingerbread man!
MUMMY: Eight hot cross buns
SOLO 2: Still warm, of course,
MUMMY: Nine ice-cream cones
SOLO 3: With chocolate sauce,
MUMMY: Ten juicy jellies topped with jam,
A hungry mummy, I am!

SOLO 4: Bring her a kipper and two lasagnes,
SOLO 1: Three macaroons with sultanas,
SOLO 2: Four nectarines ripe,
SOLO 3: Five onions and tripe,
SOLO 4: Six pasties and mince
SOLO 1: And a quiche
SOLO 2: And a quince.
SOLO 3: Eight raspberry shakes
SOLO 4: With straws, of course,
SOLO 1: Nine sirloin steaks
SOLO 2: With chasseur sauce,
SOLO 3: Ten treacle tarts with cream on top
SOLO 4: And lumpy custard,
ENSEMBLE: Yes!
MUMMY: No, stop!
(*Spoken*) Anybody got anything for indigestion?

MUSICAL SCORE – page 110

JINXED SPHINX!

DIRECTOR'S NOTES

Poor Sphinx (everyone say "Aaah!"). Well, how would you feel if your nose had fallen off? This song has an 'all-join-in' chorus.

 **SING IT.** A large singing part for the Sphinx, requiring a good memory and the ability to project pathos – singing with a peg on the nose or whilst peeling an onion may give the right sound! The **SING IT** parts of the chorus are tongue-twisters for the pyramids.

 **SAY IT.** The pyramid's **SAY IT** lines are deadpan, with an air of resignation. For thousands of years, they've stood and listened to the Sphinx as he harps on about his nasally-challenged status. Can they get up and walk away? They cannot. Oh, joy. Ask the class to script their own alternatives to help them get into character.

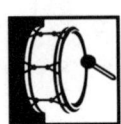 **PLAY IT.** Wood block or similar 'nose-falling-off' percussive sound!

 **TOPIC.** Pharoah Chephron's alias is Khafre. He was the son of Khufu (alias Cheops), builder of the Great Pyramid. The Granite Temple at Giza was part of Chephron's funeral site and the Second Pyramid was built for him, with the Sphinx to its right. A tall statue of Chephron, carved from diorite (dark igneous rock) stands in Cairo's Egyptian museum.

 **TOPIC.** The inscrutable Sphinx. Carved from Giza bedrock, his lion's body is 255 metres (840 feet) long and his pharoah's head is possibly a likeness of Chephron – possibly not. The body of a lion represents great strength and the Pharoah's head indicates intelligence, creating the Sphinx's combined effect of royal power. Sphinx means 'father of terror', so was he built to terrify and deter aspiring tomb-thieves?

One Sphinx legend tells of Prince Tutmosis IV, taking an afternoon nap in the Sphinx's shadow. Re, the sun-god, appeared to him in a dream, advising him to clear away the sand choking the Sphinx. If he did, a great reign awaited him. Tutmosis did as he was instructed and became king of Upper and Lower Egypt.

 **TOPIC.** The goddess Isis, to whom the Sphinx chooses to pray for the return of his own head, was known as the universal healer of ancient Egypt, following the good press she received after restoring her chopped-up husband to full health (see **Into the Light** in **Nile Style**). It was thought that she could change her heavenly form of the star, Sirius, into a bird and swoop down to earth to perform her magic. When Isis wept, the Nile flooded, embodying the waters of the Nile with divine healing properties.

THE SONG

 **SING IT.**

SPHINX:	I've been standing in the sand at Giza Since Pharoah Chephron's time.
PYRAMID 1:	(*spoken*) Here we go.
SPHINX:	When Rome was ruled by Caesar, My face was feeling fine.
PYRAMID 2:	(*spoken*) Can't imagine that.
SPHINX:	But Seth's been sending sandstorms, Erosion's taking place And my nose is down in the desert sand, It crumbled off my face.
PYRAMIDS:	He's got sand in his eyes, Sand in his ears, Sand in his . . .
SPHINX:	(*wailed*) No, that's missing!
PYRAMIDS:	The Sphinx with a jinx Prays a new nose grows, So's he can sing . . .
SPHINX:	Sand in my nose! (sobs)
PYRAMID 3:	(*spoken*) It's alright, don't cry.
SPHINX:	I've been guarding all the Pharoah's treasure, For (*sniff*) four thousand years.
PYRAMID 4:	(*spoken*) And the rest.
SPHINX:	My smile gives people pleasure, But I cry sandstone tears.
PYRAMID 5:	(*spoken*) Pass the hanky.
SPHINX:	My massive lion's body Stands twenty metres high, But my nose is down in the desert sand And that's what makes me cry.
PYRAMIDS:	He's got sand in his eyes, Sand in his ears, Sand in his . . .
SPHINX:	(*wailed*) No, that's missing!
PYRAMIDS:	The Sphinx with a jinx Prays a new nose grows, So's he can sing . . .
SPHINX:	Sand in my nose! (sobs)
PYRAMID 6:	(*spoken*) There, there.

cont.

SPHINX:	I've had a little mental crisis,
	Which Pharoah is my head?
PYRAMID 7:	(spoken) Who cares?
SPHINX:	I've asked the goddess Isis
	To bring back mine instead.
PYRAMID 8:	(spoken) Oh, no!
SPHINX:	A face with all its' features
	Would wipe away my woes,
	'Cause my nose is down in the desert sand,
	It's right between my toes.
PYRAMIDS:	He's got sand in his eyes,
	Sand in his ears,
	Sand in his . . .
SPHINX:	(wailed) No, that's missing!
PYRAMIDS:	The Sphinx with a jinx
	Prays a new nose grows,
	So's he can sing . . .
SPHINX:	Sand in my . . .
PYRAMIDS:	A-CHOO!
SPHINX:	Waaa!

MUSICAL SCORE – page 114

THE PYRAMID STOP

DIRECTOR'S NOTES

Let's rock! Let's roll! Let's finish building these pyramids before tea-break!

 **SING IT.** The opening of this song is a chain-gang chant by the slaves to create an atmosphere of hard toil. Then, the Overseer's **SING IT** turns him into an early karaoke star.

 **SAY IT.** The Slave Leader and the Overseer have a confrontational **SAY IT** as the Slave Leader insists his boys will go on strike if they have to shift one more block and the Overseer decides on his entertaining way to get them back to work.

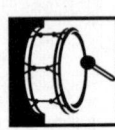 **PLAY IT.** Cymbal, crashed with feeling.

 **DRAMA.** Costume your Overseer in Elvis-style garb (see front cover) hidden under Egyptian white robes which he throws off, super-hero style, on his line "Oh yeah? Hit it!" to reveal his rock 'n' rollin' rig. If you're too young to remember Elvis, watch a video or ask the care-taker to show off his lip-curling, head-wobbling technique. On "We do the Pyramid Stop", (ideally sung by the deepest voice available, even if it's the School Secretary), everyone freezes like an Egyptian frieze – in profile.

TOPIC.   My goodness, pyramid-building was hard work. The hype was that if you helped create Pharoah's tomb, he looked out for you in the Next World. Mind you, the workers were fed, housed and clothed by the king. They were provided with linen, beer, oil, meat, fish, cheese, fruit and veg, so how bad was that? Astonishingly, Pharoah's administrators looked after up to 80,000 labourers at a time – mind-boggling logistics, even today.

Egypt's stonemasons cut limestone blocks from raw rock with copper chisels, making sure they were of the precise dimensions decreed by the architects. Blocks were numbered and marked 'this side up' to ensure their correct place in the giant jigsaw. Teams of men hauled huge blocks up ramps on wooden sledges or rollers (dampened to prevent friction fires), using papyrus ropes. Granite, ferried along the Nile from Aswan, 800 kilometres (500 miles) away, was a tougher proposition for the stonemasons. They hammered slots into the rock and drove wooden pegs into the stone. The wood was soaked until it expanded – eventually splitting the granite.

TOPIC.   The Great Pyramid at Giza took 23 years and 2,300,000 blocks to build. At 147 metres (481 feet), it's taller than St Paul's Cathedral in London and three times the height of the Statue of Liberty in New York, which stands at 46 metres (152 feet).

FX.   Get that Overseer's lash back out of the cupboard! Clapping.

THE SONG

SING IT.

SLAVES GROUP A:	We've hauled a hundred rocks today.
SLAVES GROUP B:	Ah
SLAVES GROUP A:	We've pulled a thousand blocks today.
SLAVES GROUP B:	Ah
SLAVES GROUP A:	We've walked a million miles today.
SLAVES GROUP B:	Ah
SLAVES GROUP A:	No more to roll the rocks away.
SLAVES GROUP B:	Ah
SLAVE LEADER:	STOP!
OVERSEER:	Stop?
SLAVE LEADER:	No more rocks!
OVERSEER:	No more rocks?
SLAVE LEADER:	No more roll!
OVERSEER:	Oh yeah? Hit it!

cont.

OVERSEER:	You take a limestone rock,
	You cut a limestone block.
	You do the Pyramid stamp,
	You roll it up that ramp.
	You're hauling on those ropes
	Until you reach the top.
	But when the sun goes down
	You do the Pyramid Stop.
(DANCE BREAK)	
SLAVES:	You take a limestock rock,
	You cut a limestone block.
	You do the Pyramid stamp,
	You roll it up that ramp.
	You're hauling on those ropes
	Until you reach the top.
	But when the sun goes down
	We do the Pyramid Stop!

MUSICAL SCORE – page 121

SING IT AND SAY IT (FINALE)

DIRECTOR'S NOTES

 **SING IT.** Not a lot of extra work involved here, we promise, because you and your class already know the words for the closing number because it was also the opening number.

 **DRAMA.** The repeat of the last line creates a rousing finish. We suggest a pantomime-style deep bow or similar theatrical flourish at this point before the audience storms the stage for autographs.

 **TOPIC.** Organize your class to write 30 words each, giving their impressions of this **SING IT AND SAY IT** episode. It's a very useful exercise and we always find the results fascinating. If you'd like to pass on their insights and comments to us, we'd be delighted to hear from you – and your class.

THE SONG

 **SING IT.**

ENSEMBLE: Sing it and say it, can anyone play it?
There's no need to be shy.
Sing it and say it, can anyone play it?
Come on, let's give it a try.

You'll soon learn the tune in a jiff and a half,
You'll soon learn the words, they might make you laugh!
So listen to me, there's no need to read,
Rhyme and rhythm are all you need –

 **SAY IT.**

TEACHER: Sing it with me on the count of three –
One, two, three . . .

ENSEMBLE: Four!

 **SING IT.**

ENSEMBLE: Sing it and say it, can anyone play it?
There's no need to be shy.
Sing it and say it, can anyone play it?
Come on, let's give it a,
Let's give it a,
Let's give it a try!

MUSICAL SCORE – page 126

GLOSSARY

PYRAMID	It's triangular, but it's square.
LONELY	How you feel on your first day out of college.
SMALL	How you feel on your first day out of college.
DREAM	Something you'd love to achieve – with the perfect get-out clause if you fail: "Ah well, it was only a dream." Cynical? Us?
THOUSAND	Ten times a hundred or, well, a thousand times one.
COMA	Practising for the Next World.
SAG	Succumb to the force of gravity.
THIN	A curvaceous person's dream.
CURVES	A thin person's dream.
CHIN	Your nose's shadow.
RUMBLING	Grumbling without aggression.
GRUMBLING	Rumbling with extra 'grr'.
MUMMY	Preserved parent.
KIPPER	Disgruntled herring.
MACAROON	Coconut and polystyrene biscuit.
NECTARINE	Peach with a recent shave.
TRIPE	A vegetarian's nightmare.
QUICHE	A carnivore's nightmare.
QUINCE	Fragrant fruit from a shrub of the japonica family.
SIRLOIN	Distinguished steak.
LUMPY	Smooth, having a bad day.
CUSTARD	A sweet sauce with similar consistency to wallpaper paste – well, it is in our house.
INDIGESTION	Internal re-belly-on.
SANDSTORMS	Sahara in a spin.
DESERT	Sand on holiday – there's an awful lot of it just lazing about.
SANDSTONE	Sand – in a team.
CRISIS	A situation you feel certain you'll never be able to handle. Teacher training equips you perfectly for crises.
GODDESS	A woman who thinks she knows everything. But, surely we all kn . . . ?
LIMESTONE	Posh chalk.
STAMP	Step with an added grunt.

THE PYRAMID FILE

SING IT AND SAY IT

Easily

Sing it and say it, can a-ny-one play it?__ There's no need to be shy. Sing it and say it, can a-ny-one play it?__ Come on, let's give it a try! __ You'll soon learn the tune in a jiff and a half, You'll soon learn the words, they

RIVER NILE TO GIZA

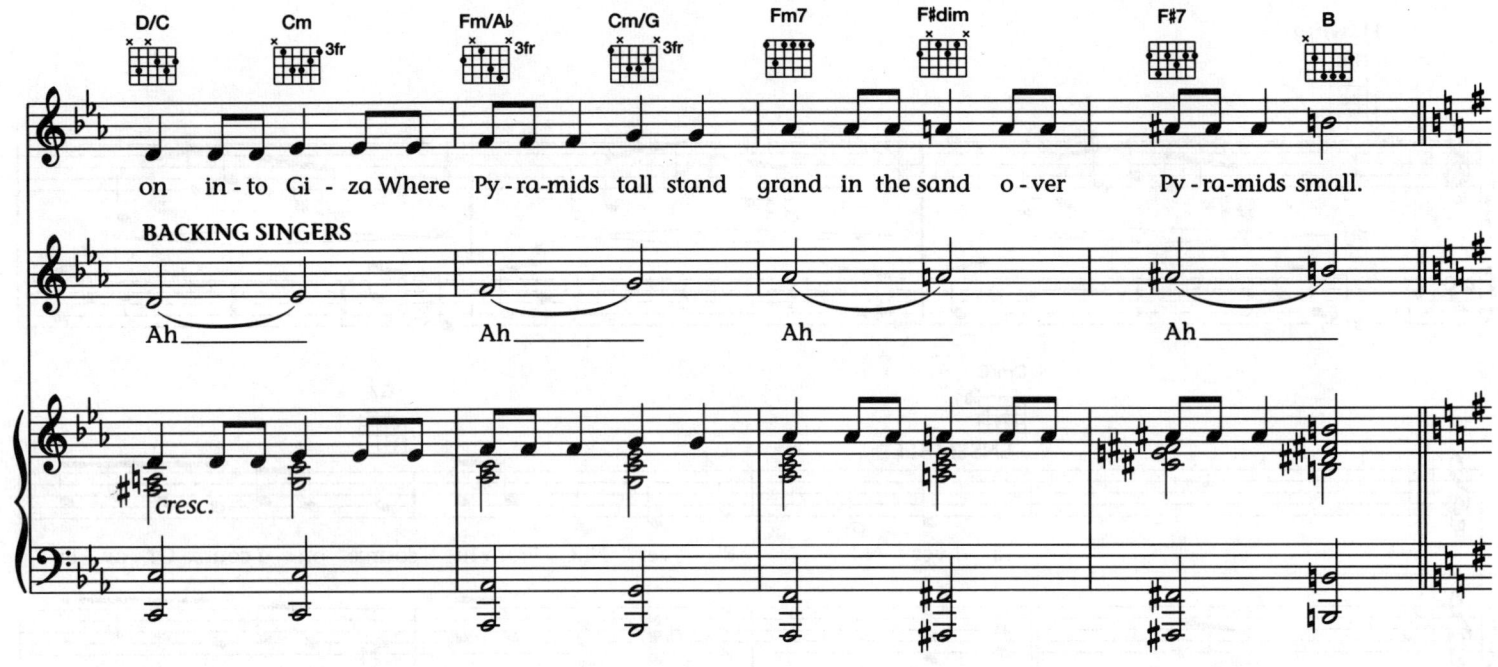

on in-to Gi-za Where Py-ra-mids tall stand grand in the sand o-ver Py-ra-mids small.

BACKING SINGERS

Ah_____ Ah_____ Ah_____ Ah_____

cresc.

SANDY SYD THE PYRAMID

In a triangular fashion

SANDY SYD

I'm

TRIANGLE

mp

San - dy Syd the Py - ra - mid.

PYRAMIDS

He's a lone - ly lit - tle

ONE HUNGRY MUMMY

With mummified grandeur – and hungry!

JINXED SPHINX

Easy tempo

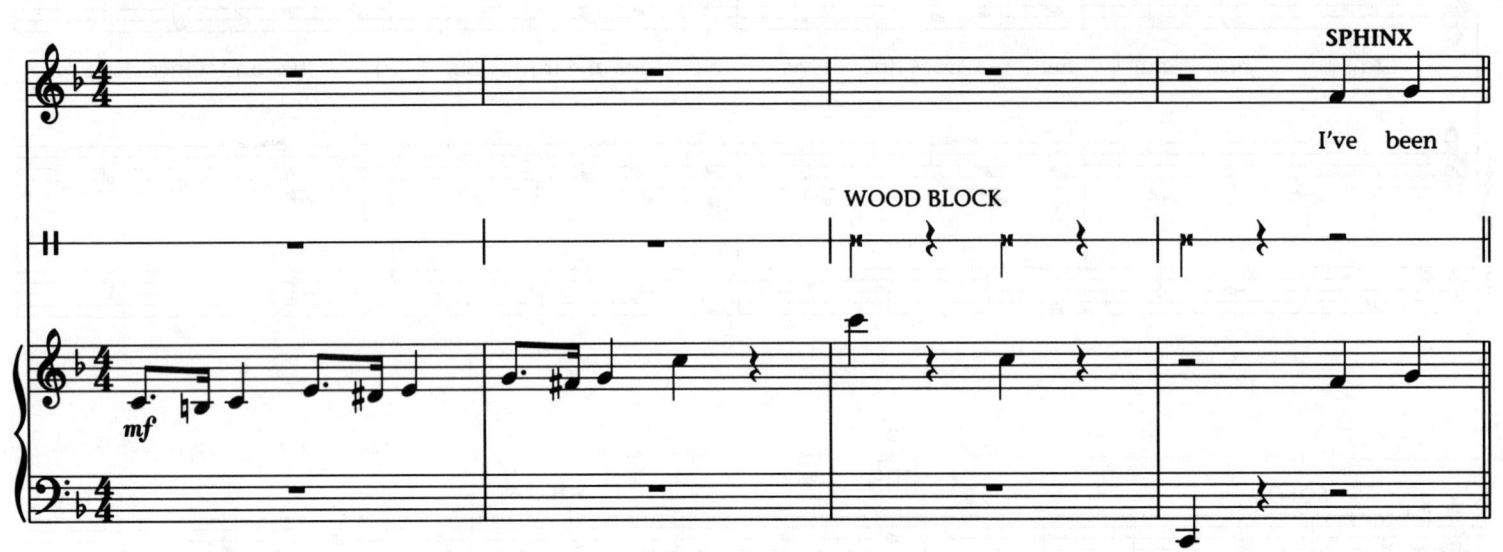

SPHINX

I've been

stand-ing in the sand at Gi - za Since Pha - roah Cheph-ron's time.

When Rome_ was_ ruled by Cae - sar, My face was feel-ing

PYRAMID 1

Here we go.

F

SPHINX

fine.　　　　　　　　　　　　But　Seth's been send-ing　sand-storms, E-

PYRAMID 2

Can't i-mag-ine that.

F7　　　　　　　Bb　　　　　　C

-ro-sion's tak-ing　place　And my　nose is down in the des-ert　sand,

It　crum-bled　off　my　face.

PYRAMIDS

He's　got

WOOD BLOCK

guard-ing all the Pha-roah's trea - sure, For *(sniff)* four thou-sand years.

My smile gives peo-ple plea - sure, But I cry sand-stone

PYRAMID 4

And the rest.

tears. My mas-sive li-on's bo-dy Stands

PYRAMID 5

Pass the han-ky.

twen-ty me-tres high, But my nose is down in the des-ert sand

THE PYRAMID STOP

sun goes down _____ You do the Py - ra-mid Stop. _____

DANCE BREAK

CLAPS

SLAVES
You take a lime-stone rock, You cut a lime-stone block. You do the

CLAPS

Py - ra-mid stamp, You roll it up that ramp. You're haul-ing on those ropes Un-til you reach the top. But when the

sun goes down_____ We do the Py - ra-mid Stop._____

ff

SING IT AND SAY IT (FINALE)

Easily

Sing it and say it, can a-ny-one play it?__ There's no need to be shy.

Sing it and say it, can a-ny-one play it?__ Come on, let's give it a try!__ You'll

soon learn the tune in a jiff and a half, You'll soon learn the words they might make you laugh! So

Printed by Halstan & Co. Ltd., Amersham, Bucks., England

8va

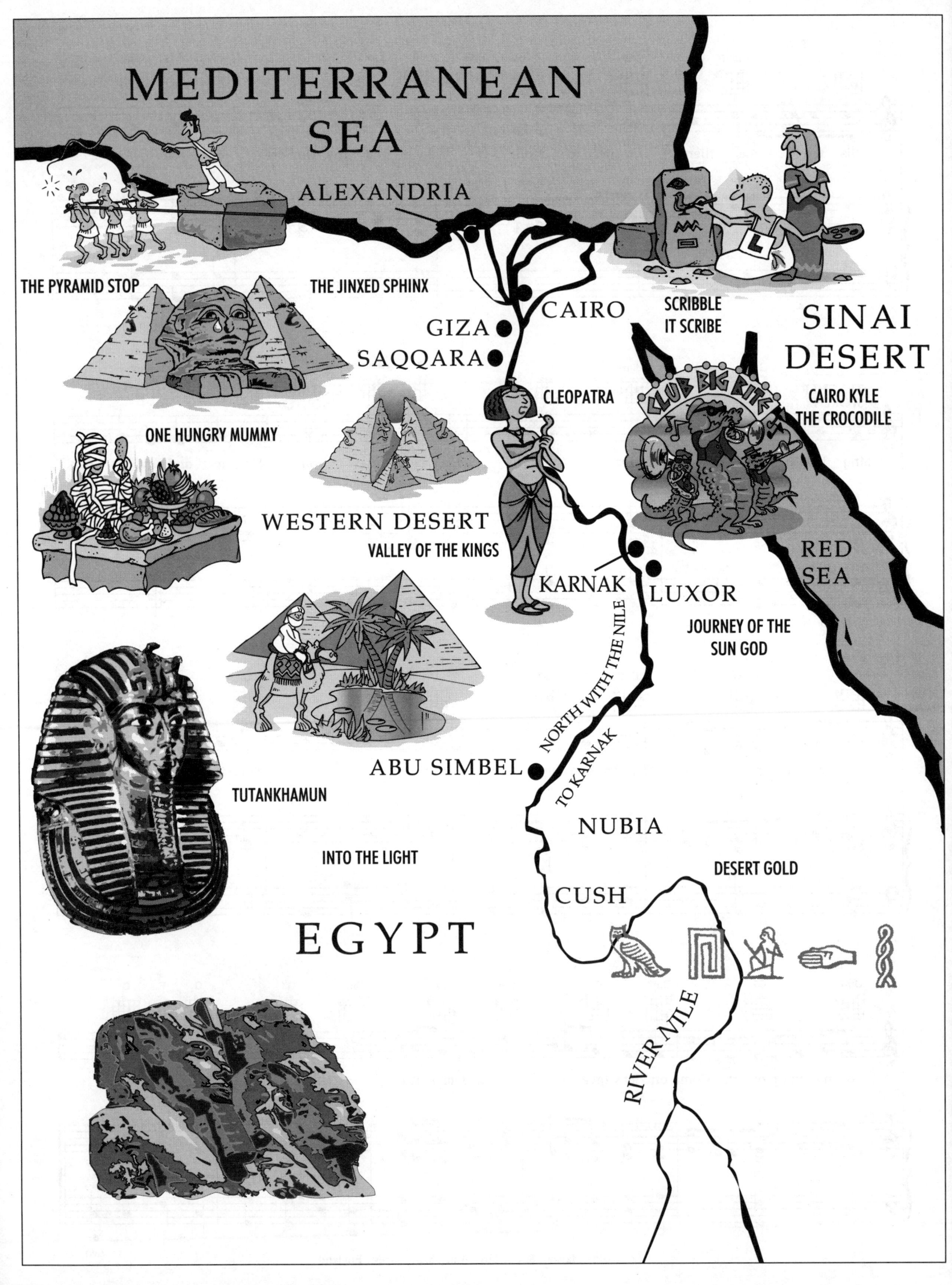